Urban Planning for Social Justice in Latin America

Urban Planning for Social Justice in Latin America explores how urban planning can be used as a tool for social equity. The book examines several Latin American cities, each with specific challenges, and explores how they have gradually overcome these difficulties through policies, planning, and design, and with private/public sector coordination.

The cases include:

- The built environment and social mobility in Bogotá;
- Mexico City and its difficulties with water scarcity;
- Addressing air quality and environmental justice in Lima;
- Santiago de Chile's energy consumption and carbon footprint;
- Buenos Aires and the issue of urban agriculture and food security;
- Connectivity as a social transformation device in Medellín.

The book goes beyond simply identifying the challenges and explains some of the practical day-to-day planning efforts, including interviews with staff from those municipalities, illustrations, and strategies that have been successful. As a result, this book will be helpful to planners in the region, as well as outside Latin America, because it demonstrates how fruitful results can be achieved in areas typically perceived as underdeveloped.

Although based on research and data, this book offers a positive perspective on the possibilities rather than the limitations, hoping to inspire new generations of planners to pursue careers in search of social change.

Camilo Espitia is a planner from Colombia. He has worked as an urban planner and designer in the private and public sectors in the United States and Latin America. He holds a master's in Engineering in Sustainable Smart Cities from University of Alabama at Birmingham, a professional bachelor's in Architecture from Florida Atlantic University, and executive education from Harvard University on Urban Retail Practices.

Urban Planning for Social Justice in Latin America

Camilo Espitia

LONDON AND NEW YORK

First published 2023
by Routledge
4 Park Square, Milton Park, Abingdon, Oxon, OX14 4RN

and by Routledge
605 Third Avenue, New York, NY 10158

Routledge is an imprint of the Taylor & Francis Group, an informa business

© 2023 Camilo Espitia

The right of Camilo Espitia to be identified as author of this work has been asserted in accordance with sections 77 and 78 of the Copyright, Designs and Patents Act 1988.

All rights reserved. No part of this book may be reprinted or reproduced or utilised in any form or by any electronic, mechanical, or other means, now known or hereafter invented, including photocopying and recording, or in any information storage or retrieval system, without permission in writing from the publishers.

Trademark notice: Product or corporate names may be trademarks or registered trademarks, and are used only for identification and explanation without intent to infringe.

British Library Cataloguing-in-Publication Data
A catalogue record for this book is available from the British Library

Library of Congress Cataloging-in-Publication Data
Names: Espitia, Camilo, author.
Title: Urban planning for social justice in Latin America / Camilo Espitia.
Description: 1 Edition. | New York, NY : Routledge, 2023. | Includes bibliographical references and index.
Identifiers: LCCN 2022056980 (print) | LCCN 2022056981 (ebook) | ISBN 9781032461359 (hardback) | ISBN 9781032462615 (paperback) | ISBN 9781003380818 (ebook)
Subjects: LCSH: City planning—Environmental aspects—Latin America. | Urban policy—Latin America. | Cities and towns—Growth. | Social justice—Latin America.
Classification: LCC HT169.L3 E867 2023 (print) | LCC HT169.L3 (ebook) | DDC 307.1/216/098—dc23/eng/20221128
LC record available at https://lccn.loc.gov/2022056980
LC ebook record available at https://lccn.loc.gov/2022056981

ISBN: 978-1-032-46135-9 (hbk)
ISBN: 978-1-032-46261-5 (pbk)
ISBN: 978-1-003-38081-8 (ebk)

DOI: 10.4324/9781003380818

Typeset in Baskerville
by Apex CoVantage, LLC

Dedication

To my grandmothers Enriqueta and Ana, my parents Hernando and Alba, Gene, my brother Gustavo, and my wife Pam. Thanks for your love and inspiration.

Contents

1 Why Latin America? 1

2 Bogotá: The Built Environment and Social Mobility 8

3 Mexico City: Infrastructure and Water for All 31

4 Lima: Air Quality and Environmental Justice 46

5 Santiago: Energy Efficiency and Sustainability 72

6 Buenos Aires: Food Security and Urban Agriculture 91

7 Medellín: (Digital) Connectivity for Social Transformation 113

8 The Future 130

Index 134

1 Why Latin America?

Introduction

In 1803, in a letter reporting on his trip to the Americas, German explorer Alexander von Humboldt wrote to his friend, Spanish taxonomic botanist Antonio José Cavanilles, that he had just arrived to "big and magnificent" Mexico City. In the same letter, Humboldt told his friend that many Europeans must have exaggerated the stories about America and its climate making it almost impossible to do research. Humboldt was not only able to do his research but was fascinated by what he encountered. He found this part of the American continent remarkable, unique, and captivating.[3] Humboldt's account is perhaps one of the first acknowledgments of the new continent's cities as equals or at least not inferior to its European counterparts.

Nonetheless, before that, the Laws of the Indies dictated the rules and management of property in the Americas, then part of the Spanish Empire. Cusco has several of its modern structures from colonial times built on top of what used to be Inca Empire institutions, such as the Convent of Santo Domingo on top of Qoricancha, the Inca's most important temple. In Lima's historic center, you can occasionally see remnants of what used to be part of the Inca Empire replaced with construction of what we see today erected by the Spanish crown.

Many of the Latin American city capitals celebrated their first century of independence in the early 1900s with investment in infrastructure with visions comparable to those of European cities. In 1949, Swiss architect Le Corbusier praised the eastern mountains of Bogotá and the greenery he saw from the airplane, only to call for a complete renovation of the city in his 1950 Plan Director, proposing Bogotá's center to be demolished and rebuilt. After both World Wars, the level of investment coming from the United States was strong enough to

DOI: 10.4324/9781003380818-1

influence new ideals of planning with car-oriented development that was applied to the growth practices of most of the Latin American capitals.

The biggest planning statements – those with the transformational force to reshape the cities of this region – assiduously docked ships and landed airplanes from distant worlds that perhaps never fully understood the place. They were seldom homegrown ideas or even constructed by or for the local population.

Social Justice

The story of how my father and grandmother arrived in a city that did not welcome or include them is the story of people who have to work twice as hard to belong and enjoy the benefits of the community. During my school years, thanks to my parents' efforts, I did not have to endure the same circumstances, but I did see firsthand how some of my classmates had to deal with them. I realized how the city was unwelcoming to them, how the city was unkind, and how the city was unjust.

Recognizing how my previous generations had arrived in and lived in the city was part of the story. The other part was the one I personally saw during my years in school. Some of my friends lived in areas where the built environment reflected their insufficient school performance. It determined their attendance, their health, and their safety. This helped to understand that the built environment, the city, its sidewalks, its parks, its buildings, and its land uses were critical to social equity.

It may be simple to recognize social justice as a contract in which society pledges the responsibility of equity for the community, but it can be slightly murky to see how that contract is executed using urban planning as one of its tools; that is, how the built environment can create connections or encourage marginalization.

Why does it matter to plan for cities that are just? How does a sidewalk create connections and represent social equity? How is zoning related to social mobility? How is the environment linked to social justice? Ensuring that cities are planned with social equity as the main goal helps to construct places that breed pride, identity, and a sense of accomplishment and belonging.

The strength of a city is not measured by its economic prowess or number of tourist destinations but by its capacity to be a place that is present for all. It is not the tallest buildings that mark its might but the kindness of the streets to its children. That kindness, the city for all, can only exist if everyone is seen as equal and if it truly belongs to everyone.

It may be that not seeing everyone as equal in Latin American cities stems from the way the cities were taken, reconstructed, developed, and recognized by the rest of the world. This, in hand, trickled into how the cities saw themselves evolving. Making sectors of the population invisible, unwelcome, or undeserving of being part of the whole could probably be both the cause and consequence of the planning and developing models used in this region for centuries.

Some of the apparently superficial issues, such as traffic congestion or narrow sidewalks, are manifestations of deeper challenges that these cities cope with. However, there are many people in the region working to make these cities just and planning for resilient environments that make these cities more inclusive and accessible to everyone. These initiatives understand their environments, acknowledge their citizens, and celebrate their local resources. It is not a matter of pride. It is a matter of survival. There is no other way these cities can move forward if not by making their local resources part of their growth. Recognizing, celebrating, and studying these initiatives will help to mobilize change, imagine new solutions, spark collaboration, and vindicate the power to shape the places people will want to live in.

To be equitable, a city needs to be adaptable and resilient. A resilient city is able to adapt and recover from sudden change, which has been typically associated with ecological and environmental impacts. However, resiliency is more than just environmentally related issues and has evolved to include sociopolitical and economic issues.[2] What is remarkable about cities in Latin America is that they operate in contexts of excessive bureaucracy and limited financial resources that are more readily available in other parts of the world; yet, the case studies in this book offer examples of good city-planning practices. All these examples are difficult to implement, take years, and in most cases are still ongoing work. However, celebrating the vision to improve the quality of life of its citizens contributes to transforming the perception of these communities. Most importantly, this vision shows that it is not only a matter of hope but of determination to improve the quality of life of millions of people.

The commitment to address water scarcity, social mobility, pollution, digital connectivity, and food security, amongst other concerns, shows the challenges and opportunities to improve livability and to build resilient cities that can better respond and recuperate from the dominant forces of potential economic, social, and environmental shocks.

4 *Why Latin America?*

As a planner in the United States, I have experienced limited budgets, disparate agendas, and, many times, discordant visions within the same community. Born and raised in Colombia, I have also had the opportunity to work in the Latin American region with very similar challenges and the same impetus of transformation. I often work with communities that, just like my parents and grandparents, arrive to places that feel hostile. However, often the global perception of this region skews their own identities, downplays the power of their transformation, and conceals some of their best qualities.

The Case Studies

Through personal research, interviews, and experiences, the book aims not only to celebrate these efforts but to inspire change in other cities around the planet and to shift the position these cities have on the collective mental map outside the region. The Latin American city has the capacity of transformation with its own resources; after all, it was in these urban centers that the independentist movements were born, and new ideas are stronger as a network than on their own; thus, sharing ideas and concepts is vital.

This book focuses on the solutions, not on the problems, but it does understand that solutions come from assessing the challenges. These cities understand their potential and use the opportunity to use their own natural and human resources to intertwine them with their urban development. They are added value and certainly not an obstacle.

To begin the conversation of resiliency in Latin American cities, we need to look at their origins as urban centers and understand part of the background that forged their present and their aspirations to transform themselves in the future.

Today, 80 percent of the population in Latin America lives in cities, and according to data from the United Nations Economic Commission for Latin America (CEPAL), some countries in the region will reduce their populations by 2100, some will be even more urbanized, and some will get older.[1] But even if the predictions do not hold true, the case studies in this book describe a vision to take charge of what these cities want to become.

Even though the research for this book began in 2017, the COVID-19 pandemic exposed some of the problems these cities face every day and provided a window to that future if resiliency and adaptability are not part of the vision. While, in some instances, clean air gave way to healthier environments and positive ecological side-effects during the quarantine period, in others, the inability to access housing, health care, technological connectivity, economic opportunities, and food security confirmed the inequality in the region. This worldwide event emphasized the need to include economic, environmental, and social resiliency in development programs and to continue the support and strengthening of policies that can better adapt and respond for the well-being of its citizens. Several cities in the region have started implementing agendas that strive for better, livable environments.

Latin American cities used to be in the passenger seat of the dialogue on planning, innovation, technology, equality, trade, and resources management. As its urban population grew, so did its problems: every day saw a combination of poverty, inequality, pollution, chaos, and ad-hoc growth that created environments where opportunities were lost, pollution made residents sick, and segregation grew.

Discordant political climates in the region and the burden of uncontrolled population growth triggered the necessity to become the drivers of that conversation on their own terms and with their own resources. Cities like Medellín became examples of the impossible made possible, Curitiba inspired Bogotá with the rapid bus-transit system, and Bogotá inspired New York with the temporary closure of roads to create bicycle lanes. Chile is a world pioneer-actor in energy efficiency and management.

No longer did these cities need to exclusively look toward the Global North to find their vision for the future. That vision was possible with their own ideas and their own mechanisms. In some cities, their origins were the answer. In others, catastrophes pushed them forward. But that takes time. And, although these cities keep evolving, they are fully matured and their maturity comes with an acknowledgment of their own flaws. The questions of how to address these imperfections have involved forward-thinking policy makers, experts in different fields, the academic world, and the citizenry in the dialogue, and the determination devoted to changing their fate.

The cities in this book were chosen because each of them has been intentionally invested in addressing its specific challenges as a result of understanding the necessity to improve social justice. I have visited or worked in some of the cities or, in some instances, have relied on research at a distance, along with interviews with local experts to understand their success or simply highlight the goals aimed at, even if they still are in progress. Some of the cities in the book have urban laboratories (LabCDMX, LabCapital, and ViveLab in Bogotá; Laboratorio de Gobierno in Chile; or Subsecretaría de Innovación Pública y Gobierno Abierto in Argentina; and Ruta N in Medellín) that have

6 Why Latin America?

begun cooperation efforts to share knowledge and have offered lessons learned as part of their experimentation processes.[4]

Every chapter of this book talks about the problems of urban development connected to a social topic. To reduce the negative impact of social injustice, these cities tackle public health issues, hunger, social mobility, water scarcity, pollution, and the digital divide through urban development strategies.

The emergency of water resources, the capacity of zoning to impact people's ability to move up the socioeconomic ladder, or the effect of transportation and energy consumption on air quality and the carbon footprint of cities live silently in the back of people's minds. In the meantime, more tangible subjects, such as safety perception or traffic congestion, occupy the headlines of the news. It is not that those topics are not important. It is that they are consequences of deeper issues in city planning and development, which helps provide a framework that is discussed in the book.

A common trend in the selection of these case studies is that, after years of migration into these cities and unplanned urbanization, the process has forged social inequity, pollution, and resource challenges due to overpopulation, with considerable spatially marked differences.

This book starts with Bogotá, addressing land use and zoning and their effect on social mobility and the latest master plan the city will be implementing for the upcoming decades. This first chapter includes data gathered through a survey distributed digitally to several residents in the city.

Then, the discussion moves to Mexico City to consider the pressing matter of water resources. One of the most populated cities in the world is having water challenges that have implications beyond supply. Many residents receive low-quality water, and the depletion of its aquifers has an effect on the city's underground structure. This chapter discusses what Mexico City is doing to mitigate its water-supply exhaustion.

After that, the discussion moves to Lima to address air quality and how it is impacted by the city's growth and its geographic location. This chapter describes the consequences of poor air quality and some of the policies Lima is implementing to overcome the issue.

After that, on to Santiago to explore how it has handled development and energy consumption to mitigate the city's carbon footprint and how it has become a pioneer in the region to reduce consumption and improve its sustainable energy sources.

Next is Buenos Aires with the topic of food production and security. The city is currently having issues with food security for a sector of the population – an issue that was exacerbated by the COVID-19 pandemic. The chapter explains some the strategies implemented to improve food access.

Finally, the book closes with Medellín – which went from being one of the most dangerous cities in the world in the 1980's to one of inclusion policies through urban-design strategies to then become an innovation hub – this time addressing the topic of information and connectivity and its impact on the social transformation of the city.

While no single process will work in the entire region, these case studies illustrate several successful tactics that other cities can use. At the very least, they shed light on a different perspective on these cities, allowing us to bear witness to their challenges, but most importantly, to their power of change.

References

1 CEPAL. (2022) *Estimaciones y Proyecciones: Archivos Excel.* Comisión Económica para América Latina y el Caribe: Washington, DC.
2 Coaffee, J. and Lee, P. (2016) *Urban Resilience: Planning for Risk, Crisis and Uncertainty.* Palgrave: London/New York.
3 Humbolt, A. (1989) *Cartas Americanas. Alexander Humbolt* (Charles Minguet (editor), Marta Traba (translator)). Biblioteca Ayacucho: Caracas, Venezuela.
4 Laboratorio Para La Ciudad. (2017) *Ciudad Posible. Primer Encuentro de Laboratorios Urbanos de America Latina.* https://labcd.mx/experimentos/ciudad-posible-primer-encuentro-de-laboratorios-urbanos-de-america-latina/. Accessed December 14, 2020.

2 Bogotá
The Built Environment and Social Mobility

People ran everywhere; others looted and destroyed property; while others burned streetcars in the riots ignited by the assassination of Jorge Eliecer Gaitán, the front-runner of the upcoming 1949 Colombian presidential elections. The riots were the manifestation of the social frustrations from decades before, and that fatal Friday April 9, 1948, now known as the "Bogotazo," initiated one of the most brutal decades of Colombia in the years after, known as "La Violencia." The trolley cars that arrived in the second decade of the twentieth century were set on fire, overturned, and 34 cars were completely destroyed, representing over 30 percent of the fleet.[18] Although the City purchased new streetcars to replace some of the ones lost during the protests, regular bus services were already part of the transportation system of Bogotá, and the restoration of the streetcar system was deemed financially impossible, accelerating the dismantling of the service. Thus, buses and trolleybuses began replacing the streetcars. La Violencia, the civil war triggered by El Bogotazo, spread and intensified throughout the countryside, pushing people to Bogotá, more than doubling its population in the next decade: from 648,424 people in 1951 to 1,697,311 in 1964.[55]

In 1938, to commemorate the 400th anniversary of Bogotá's foundation, the city built its largest roadway infrastructure project, known as "Avenida Caracas," to connect and reintegrate informal neighborhoods that were the signs of the uncontrolled sprawl of the city.[2] This major project, intended to extend the connectivity of Bogotá, fell short in comparison to the growth rate of the city, and transportation became a large necessity. Development went mostly north-south following the Avenida Caracas axis as a compass.[14] By the 1950s, the inclusion of several municipalities in the city's administrative footprint made transportation a primary need for the city, surpassing that of sewage, water, and electricity. This disconnected the population from services and intensified the inequalities of the city.[44]

DOI: 10.4324/9781003380818-2

Transportation and mobility entered a crisis. "La Guerra del Centavo" (The Cent War) during the 1970s and 1990s left several injuries and fatalities due to bus drivers who – without salaries and relying on the number of passengers picked up throughout the day for their income – recklessly drove the streets of Bogotá.

It was around this time that I began riding public transportation to school on my own. My school was a public facility without its own transportation system, about 11 kilometers from where we lived. It was at school where I began to realize that many of my classmates had no other option but to walk longer distances from different parts of the city to get to school, often more than the 11 kilometers of my bus ride. On foot.

Many of my classmates came from underserved areas with sidewalks in very poor conditions or no sidewalks at all. Others could not afford lunch on our break, while others had to work after school to help their families pay rent. Because of school-group projects, I went to many of my classmates' homes and neighborhoods. This is when I began understanding the concept of social layers and the differences between several of my classmates and the disconnections in the city, both physically and socially. It was not until years later that I would understand my bus rides and my friends' living conditions as the manifestations of the problems the city had with equality and access to opportunities for many of its citizens and their relationship to the built environment.

Why did we have to go so far to attend school?[23] Why was public transportation so precarious? Why was the city organized this way? Why did ten-year-old children have to work to contribute to their households? Why did some houses and their neighborhoods look the way they did, and why were certain buildings located where they were?

In this chapter, we will look at an overview of how cities around the globe are shaped and the link between built environment and social mobility and why it is important. We will then explore the development of Bogotá and how it has defined the land structure in the city. We will show overall results from a survey conducted for this chapter. We will explain the effects that the land structure's built system has on social mobility in Bogotá; we will elaborate on the importance of improving these numbers; and we will examine what Bogotá is doing to promote this.

The Shape of Cities Around the World

Most cities developed using their natural surroundings as their ground rule. That meant that topography, climate, water sources, and food sources dictated the extents, methods, and layouts of their footprints. Some have endured through thousands of years, like Damascus in Syria, while others have disappeared, like Tikal from the Mayan civilization. Their forms have also shifted as they grow and environmental and economic challenges have triggered social ones. As they become more globalized, issues like immigration[15] and political weight on the international stage become more evident. However, their adjustments to development have differed throughout regions and continents.

While in Europe, according to Maarten van Ham, coauthor of *Spatial Segregation and Socio-Economic Mobility in European Cities*[60], there are differences in segregation levels amongst European cities, depending on the location and concentration of low-cost housing; in Latin America, the common trend is a peripheral, sprawling socioeconomic segregation, which also differentiates it from the way North American cities evolved.[3, 31]

In the United States, people with the economic capacity and encouraged by racial division, segregating policies, and the disinvestment of city cores moved to the peripheries of cities[16] to what they considered better living conditions in a period known as "white flight." In Latin America, immigrants from within the country, especially rural areas, moved as close as possible to the economic opportunities offered by cities, even if it meant moving to land unsuitable for development, mostly at the periphery of the city.[25, 41] The farther from the center people had to go, the harder it was to access the centers of employment and education that they came looking for in the city, intensifying the socioeconomic gap between those parts of the city. This pattern holds true for most of the region.[38, 58]

In China, many of the recently built cities are investor projects where the rate of development is faster than the rate at which the population manages to occupy these cities. The large, fast real estate investments end up empty for months before people begin moving in. But even before these modern times, many Chinese cities have been deliberately planned and established following different organizational and hierarchal principles throughout their history. The first main governmental and religious centers in China were planned and built as protected, walled towns.[32]

Islamic cities were built to encourage social gathering to promulgate and live Islam. They were characterized by Mahallas, which were neighborhoods that typically ended in smaller courtyards or plazas, where some of them acted as smaller administrative subdivisions of the city. This system of smaller plazas creates a sense of collectivity and belonging by strong socioreligious principles.[54]

Bogotá 11

It is not that none of the cities with other structures and development patterns do not experience the same social afflictions or that they have not suffered from catastrophes that have forced change. American and European cities also suffer from segregation issues, immigration, or infrastructure-investment challenges. It is simply that their geometries define different built environments that have an effect on the quality of life of communities in different ways.

Bogotá has been an incidental evolution of a radial pattern, where beyond the center there were no rules, and the growth of the city pushed people further from the core, alienating them from services, opportunities, and social advantages. Worst of all, the built environment can perpetuate the alienation and the possibility for people to recuperate from their socioeconomic adversities.[29, 30]

How Does the Built Environment Affect Social Mobility?

Social mobility is the link between an individual's socioeconomic status growing up in their family and their position as an adult.[33] Measurements of social mobility gauge the capacity of individuals to access opportunities and move upward in the social scale and help to indicate whether a place provides such opportunities. Evidently, social mobility is dependent on several factors that include education, employment, and health care, to name a few; but in this chapter, we will focus on the urban built environment because it is the one tool planners have the ability to improve the connectivity to those services, including providing spaces that are healthier and contribute to social capital through planning and zoning.

Social and cultural capital, influences of the early years, education, employment, health and well-being, and physical and built-environment influences are all factors that have an effect on social mobility.[45] These factors manifest themselves in cities in the form of employment hubs, housing affordability, access to quality educational centers, physical activity, clean and safe environments, and transportation[57] (accessibility of such services). In terms of social capital, epidemiologist Soumya Mazumdar, in the 2017 research *The Built Environment and Social Capital*, provided evidence for the relationship between the quality of the built environment and social wealth.[42] Communities with spaces to exchange collective interests establish cultural ties that construct social capital. These interactions happen in public spaces such as sidewalks, services such as stores, banks, and public parks, as well as in community centers, houses of worship, and schools, showing that there are positive relationships between the level of accessibility of civic space and social cohesion.

Public areas also have a positive effect on social mobility in their capacity to provide zones for improving health. A 2016 study on physical activity and the link to the built environment in several cities around the world, which included Bogotá, found that parks are closely related to adult physical activity and demonstrated that open areas provide zones for exercise, leisure, and transportation hubs that contribute to increased physical activity.[53] Furthermore, health can be linked to the built environment in the form of affordable and quality housing. Not only does inadequate housing affect physical health through issues such as respiratory problems, but it can also lead to toxic stress, which triggers mental complications[46] that can cause long-term damage.[12]

Another physical trait that affects social mobility is housing affordability and ownership. Zoning often affects housing affordability by restricting housing production and supply, which not only reduces access to adequate housing and decent living conditions but also hinders homeownership.[36] This is concerning because homeownership contributes to the accumulation of equity and wealth, which, according to OECD (2018), parents often use to invest in their children's education and serves as an inheritance. At the same time, homeownership affects the accessibility to employment centers as seen in Figure 2.1.

Connectivity in the form of transportation is critical because it provides access to employment, educational institutions, and other services in cities that do not have a compact design that allows for mixed uses. Proper mobility in a city translates into more social and economic opportunities.

Why Is It Important for Cities to Provide Tools for Social Mobility?

With more than 80 percent of global GDP coming from cities (World Bank, 2019) and government structures becoming more specialized and localized, entire nations depend on providing these population centers with the tools to build a more socially and economically resilient environment, because without the flexibility of social mobility, the regeneration mechanisms that give life to society will disappear.[28]

In the second half of the twentieth century, governments in Latin America relinquished the focus on social mobility to address the urgency of poverty.[28] However, the general economic expansion of the region in the decade of the 1990s opened avenues for research on social structures and inequality. Today, governments have begun paying attention to urban centers and their socioeconomic compositions, as they have become large production nodes[50] where, according to the Atlantic Council Adrianne Arsht Latin American Center, 80 percent of the population live in cities, generating 60 percent of the region's GDP.

Today, the region has recently improved efforts to measure social mobility; for example, Mexico did so with the 2006 and 2011 Surveys on Social Mobility in Mexico (EMOVI 2006, 2011). In the United Mexican States, upward social mobility in Mexico City is greater than in any other region of the country.[47] This makes it a place where, despite great economic and social inequalities, the population still finds better opportunities for promotion on the socioeconomic ladder than any other city in the country.

In Argentina, after the 2001–2002 economic crisis, the country introduced modifications to its economic policies, which had a positive influence on its socioeconomic structures.[22] Not surprisingly, Buenos Aires, as the capital and city with the largest percentage of population and productivity in the country (according to the 2010 National Census, Buenos Aires represented 32 percent of the country's population and 40 percent of its GDP), has the greatest social mobility compared to other cities and regions within Argentina. However, even though the decade of the 2000s (after the economic crisis) showed improvement in the numbers of absolute mobility (improvement in mobility for society as a whole compared to the previous generation due to higher incomes and the value of currency), relative mobility (comparison of the movement of individuals from different socioeconomic levels) did not show great improvement compared to prior decades.[49]

In Africa, another region with socioeconomic challenges, research on Intergenerational Mobility in Africa provided evidence of the relationship between the higher investment in infrastructure, more developed urban habitat, and improved social mobility numbers.[1]

In areas of the world with low social mobility, increasing those opportunities for success not only benefits those on lower socioeconomic groups but cities as a whole. A strong socioeconomic mobility contributes to social equity and overall prosperity for entire countries and regions.[24]

Land Structure in Bogotá

From the native Chibcha word Bacatá, which means "sowing fields," comes the name of the capital of Colombia: Bogotá. Founded in 1538, the city has transformed mostly as a self-organized urban system through its nearly five centuries.

With 7.2 million residents as of the 2018 national census, the city covers a territory of 1,775 km² with a density of 4,056 people/km². Sprawl in Bogotá has created challenges of accessibility to employment centers,[40] precarious housing, and limited access to water, sewage, green open spaces, transportation, and educational institutions, which translates into lower educational levels, limited employment opportunities, unhealthy environments, and low social capital, affecting social mobility. Part of the horizontal development of the city has been driven by land speculation and housing affordability problems[51] that are intrinsically related to the informality in which the city grew,[34] since this is how many of its low-income residents had a chance at living and being part of the city.[13]

Between 1950 and 2010, about 21 percent of the urbanized surface of Bogotá's territory was illegally generated by people migrating to areas that were not residential zones or prepared for residential development.[13] Most of the illegal development happened in the south or at the eastern periphery of the city. Figure 2.1 shows the density of development around the axis of Avenida Caracas that includes employment and more mixed-use developments, indicating the separation between the mostly residential areas of the city and those with the services and employment.

The primary mode of informal settling in Bogotá is a consequence of illegal (not allowed by zoning) lot subdivisions contributing to low-quality, self-built neighborhoods. This problem is dominated by "*tierreros*," or land dealers, who buy land from owners who cannot develop the land (due to zoning regulations) and see more profit in selling than using it for agriculture. Tierreros then illegally subdivide the land and sell it to underprivileged people looking for affordable land with informal credit accommodations, using a buyer-seller promise contract as the only legal document, instead of a notarized property title or deed. Slowly, these development trends have shaped the city into segregated areas with different urban accommodations and social classes, called *estratos* in Colombia, with most of the periphery on the southern edge of the city housing the lower income population.[7]

Figure 2.2 shows the geographical distribution of *estratos* in the city. The black and dark gray areas show *estratos* 6 and 5, respectively, mostly

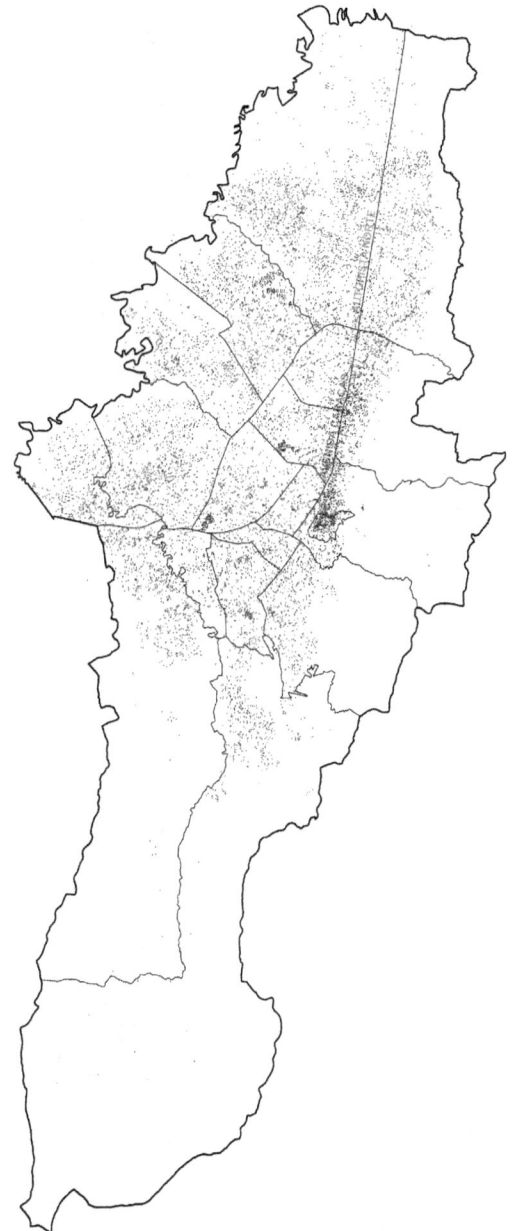

Figure 2.1 Bogotá Development Density by Camilo Espitia
Source: Based in Information from Datos Abiertos Bogotá.

16 *Bogotá*

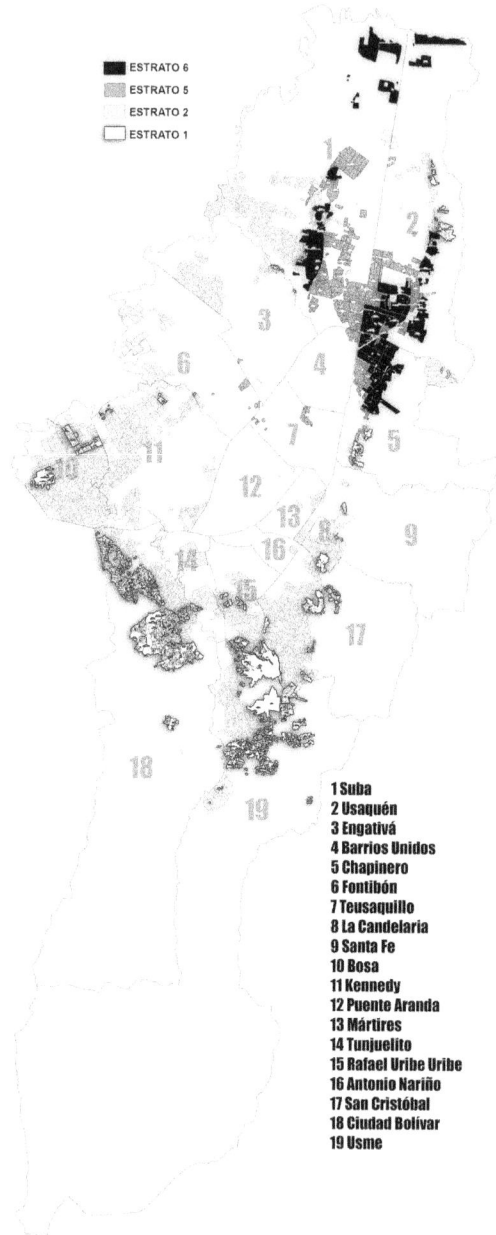

Figure 2.2 Social Layers Map by Camilo Espitia
Source: Datos abiertos Bogotá.

found toward the north of the city and adjacent to the main axis of development, known as Avenida Caracas (which becomes Autopista Norte as it moves north). The white and light gray areas represent *estratos* 1 and 2 respectively, which are mostly found on the periphery of the city, predominantly toward the south.

Most of these areas were informal settlements at some point that have slowly been formalized into the official urban footprint of the city, but have not necessarily received formal investment in infrastructure. In other words, even though they are now official blocks that are categorized as "urbanized," and for which there are deed titles on the national registry, they still lack proper urban infrastructure, such as access to transportation, sidewalks, public lighting, or public spaces. And, while that official transition happens, informal development in Bogotá means that the owner of a plot of land not only does not obtain basic services or infrastructure, but the real estate value cannot be used as a capital investment, source of equity, or wealth accumulation. Without recognition by official institutions, be it the government or private entities like banks, the owners cannot use them as equity to secure loans for home improvements, tertiary education for their children, or enterprising. This also represents additional costs to the city during the legalization and improvement phases of these areas that could be phased throughout their development. It simply indicates that the growth of the city has outstripped its planning.

It was not until the year 2000 that Bogotá established its first Territorial Organizational Plan (POT) with a development plan that integrated economic, social, and environmental concepts in the growth of the city. Some of the topics addressed in this plan include transit-oriented development that allows taller buildings around major transportation nodes, alternative modes of mobility, reduced parking requirements, connectivity to surrounding municipalities, the Bogotá River as an integrating axis within and outside Bogotá, increased number of protected green areas, the preservation of the Van der Hammen Reserve, and the targeting of an increase in housing development to mitigate the demand and potentially reduce housing costs. This basically means that land would be enabled to develop affordable housing, increase the ability to develop mixed uses while mitigating the impact of higher density development – integrating the natural resources into the public system implementation – and build a walkable, compact, denser city.

In 2021, a Bogotá-Region plan was approved in the Senate to address development in the city and its surrounding communities outside its administrative boundaries as a regional coordinated effort. One of the characteristics of this new plan is the mobility's focus shift from

Transmilenio to the Metro, Regiotram – connecting these municipalities, gondolas, and green corridors – and more bicycle lanes.

What are *estratos* in Colombia?

The socioeconomic layers in Bogotá are defined as *estratos*, which are established by criteria derived from the quality of the construction of a home and several other factors of the built environment, including the surrounding neighborhood of the property. But what are *estratos*? Decree 969 of 1991 (House of Nariño Office) established a method of categorizing each residential unit in urban settings to allocate utility pricing based on their physical characteristics, the availability of utilities, the condition of adjacent roads and other elements of infrastructure, access to recreational facilities and green areas, quality of transportation, and the concentration of commercial uses around the home. Later, Law 142 of 1994 created the subsidy system that required higher income groups to help fund services such as sewage, telephone, power, gas, and waste management for lower socioeconomic groups.[39] The system is divided into six layers, with layer 1 being the most limited housing conditions, and 6 the least limited.

The measuring unit for socioeconomic layer distribution is the city block. In certain cases, where some properties are extremely different from the rest of the properties within the block, a specific layer is assigned to such property. Another factor pertaining to the division of layers based on the condition of the physical aspects of properties is their home value appreciation in the long term; after all, lower *estratos* show lower property appreciation (which affects the accumulation of generational wealth) than those of higher *estratos* according to the 2010 Sistema Tributario del Distrito Capital (2010 Capital District Property Tax System).

Social Mobility Numbers in Bogotá

Even though "*estrato*" classification in all Colombian cities is based on the examination of the built environment, the built environment is generally a manifestation of household economic conditions, which are a reflection of employment status, income levels, and educational achievement and performance. According to the 2013 Bogotá Social Mobility Index Bulletin No. 58 from the Bogotá Secretary of Planning, children's future opportunities are affected by their parents' income and education level. In Bogotá, the educational factor indicates a general tendency toward stagnation in terms of the educational levels

Table 2.1 Conceptual Mobility Possibilities by Camilo Espitia, Based on the 2013 Bogotá Social Mobility Index Bulletin

Estrato	Social Mobility Opportunity
6 Highest	MINIMUM
5	LOW
4	**HIGH**
3	**HIGH**
2	LOW
1 Lowest	MINIMUM

achieved from one generation to the next, where educational mobility is only higher in *estratos* 3 and 4. The report shows that the lowest mobility numbers are present among both the lowest and highest socioeconomic groups in the city: while the lower *estratos* experience less upward mobility, previous generations with high education and income indicators tend to have children who will also achieve that level.[56] (Essentially, these individuals cannot climb any higher on the socioeconomic ladder, and it is unlikely that they will move lower.) Within the six socioeconomic levels, the middle levels (groups three and four) have more opportunities for mobility (see Table 2.1).

Access to education is critical to social mobility. Research has shown that, despite some differences between the countries in the context of the entire Latin American region, higher educational levels are visibly linked to higher incomes, demonstrating the importance of access to education.[43] According to the *Intergenerational Social Mobility in Latin America: A Review of Existing Evidence* study that examined the link between parents' education and their children's schooling in urban settings (0, no correlation; 1, full correlation), Colombia had a coefficient of almost 0.65, higher than Peru and Mexico (both at 0.5) and the United States (0.35). Thus, on average, Colombia has poor social mobility, at almost 60 percent of children with the tendency to maintain the same level as their parents.[5]

A major challenge is school dropout rates, which remain high in urban settings in Latin America. According to Diana María Moreno Bernal and her 2013 study *School Desertion: A Social Character Problem*, in urban centers of Colombia, the school desertion rate in 2002 was 20 to 25 percent. This is considered average in the Latin American region, with countries like Honduras and Guatemala reporting rates of 40 and 70 percent, respectively, though Bolivia, Chile, and Peru had rates below 20 percent.[9] Bogotá, in particular, has shown improvement in reducing school abandonment rates in recent years.

According to a 2018 study from the Bogotá Secretary of Education, in 2015, 28,000 children quit school in the city, while in 2017, the number fell to less than 12,000. Nevertheless, out of this 12,000, 29 percent reported that their primary reason for quitting school was that it was too far from their place of residence. This supports the argument that spatial conditions play a critical role in education access, and by extension, in social mobility.

The role of territorial ordinances (zoning) in Bogotá is an important factor in determining the number and location of educational institutions, which affects how far students must travel and how convenient they are to access. The location of public educational facilities in Colombia, for many years, was linked to the concepts of how to educate the population in settings separate from the daily troubles and distractions of urban life. Schools were placed out of urban settings to better regulate their surroundings.[59] Hence, for generations, schools were inconveniently located and hard to access, often via school buses. Not until the first decades of the twenty-first century did the location of schools become an integral part of zoning ordinances linked with the educational system in terms of provisions, locations, quantities, equipment, and services such as transportation and nutrition. Article 7 from the 2006 Bogotá Educational Institutions Master Plan refers to the need to develop schools within the urban framework of the city's development, focusing on the setting of collective spaces.[11] As of 2016, Bogotá had 2,400 schools, with only 29 in rural settings.

In overall social mobility, a 2013 study from the Secretary of Planning in Bogotá reported that areas with the lowest mobility are Ciudad Bolivar, Chapinero, Usme, and La Candelaria. Geographically speaking, the lowest mobility (except Chapinero, an area with low mobility simply because it is already of the highest *estrato*) coincide with those areas with lower *estratos*, which are those with transportation, infrastructure, and safety issues. The localities of Usme and Ciudad Bolivar, located on the periphery and southern edges of the city, were large farms that began illegal subdivisions to accommodate the growing population during the 1950s. Today, these localities still suffer from a lack of urban infrastructure that hinders connectivity to the rest of the city.

In my conversation with Andrea Baena, an architectural and urban designer from Bogotá, Colombia with experience in the Latin American region with a masters in Architecture from MIT in Boston and a bachelors in Industrial Engineering from Universidad de los Andes, she agrees. Andrea stated, "The built environment has a high impact on social mobility. For example, in Bogotá, low-cost housing development occurs predominantly on the outskirts of the city where the cost of land is lower and connections to areas of economic opportunity are limited. Therefore, the citizens of these low-cost homes have a disadvantage compared to others located in areas that are better connected to work places or educational institutions. This generates a vicious cycle that reduces social mobility" (Baena, A., personal communication, November 4, 2022).

Survey, Existing Research, and Relationship to Findings

As part of my research for this chapter during 2019, a survey [4, 6, 8, 17, 20, 21, 27, 37, 48, 52] was distributed to several residents in Bogotá to understand firsthand the changes in mobility in conjunction with physical urban factors. The survey asked questions about their socioeconomic status, educational level, gender, age, employment, housing and neighborhood quality, safety, proximity to services, transportation, and community engagement and compared those results to their parents to understand the generational changes in all those factors.

The questionnaire was sent to 1,002 people, divided by the six established "estratos" for a total of 167 people per "*estrato*". The survey revealed that, even with higher educational mobility, social mobility is limited in the city. This finding strengthens the thesis of the effect of the city's expansion and land use and zoning ordinances in influencing its low rates of social mobility.

The answers related to respondents' present conditions and those of their parents (or previous generation), support a comparative description on the living conditions of both generations and the relationship to the built environment. Issues such as transportation, entertainment and public venues, education access, public spaces, and public participation and engagement, in general, differ very little from one generation to the next. In fact, the change in "*estrato*" shown in this survey matches the trends reported by the 2013 Bogotá Social Mobility Index Bulletin No. 58, with the majority of mobility concentrated in "*estratos*" 3 and 4.

The survey revealed a generational reduction in employment status, which is essential for higher incomes that directly affect social mobility. These results also may be a reflection of the informality of the job market in both the city and the country in general, which affects access to a consistent income and increases the difficulty of financial commitments such as loans and credit. Informality is characterized by either not having an actual employment contract or not receiving benefits.

Involvement in community groups and the perception of safety in respondents' neighborhoods also decreased from one generation to the next. This is important because community belonging is an important element to build social capital,[35] which in hand is critical for social mobility. What is important about this aspect is that community involvement is supported by a built environment that encourages people's interaction with better sidewalks, parks, public spaces, and cultural amenities, all shaped through urban planning.

Homeownership, one of the largest forms of wealth accumulation,[10,26] also shows a decrease across generations in the survey. In regards to the housing typology, there was an increase in the rate of apartments compared to the previous generation. These results are related to the issue of homeownership, where more people are living in rented units, which are mostly apartments. A 2018 study on housing affordability in Colombia by the National Association of Financial Institutions (ANIF) found that 44 percent of households in Colombia rent their homes. This may be a reflection of the reduction in size of the typical household in the country, but it also touches on the subject of home ownership affordability in Bogotá, which has one of the most expensive real estate markets in the country, affecting mostly the lower "*estratos.*"

While multi-unit development for rent means that there is more supply of housing, which can presumably translate into more affordable housing, it can also mean that there is less opportunity for home ownership.

The survey also showed little improvement in housing and neighborhood conditions. This is troubling, because not only is housing quality an economic asset, but it represents a threat to physical and mental health issues,[19] including those arising from communities with safety concerns, lack of open spaces, or poor connectivity.

The survey showed a limited presence of mixed-use development, including office uses, businesses, and commerce (uses that represent employment opportunities) for both generations. It also revealed the difficulty of access to schools, as well as entertainment and cultural facilities. This aligns with a 2017 study by the Development Bank of Latin America, called "Urban Growth and Access to Opportunities: A Challenge for Latin America"[61], which indicates the differences between the formal and informal city, including access to services, schools and amenities. The findings in this survey align with the study and reveal the concerns of Bogotá's development as an informal metropolis where a sector of the population lacks critical services, limiting economic opportunities and social capital essential to upward social mobility. Table 2.2 shows an overview of the survey and the differences between the respondents and their previous generation.

Table 2.2 Survey Results by Camilo Espitia

Parents/Previous Generation	Respondant
FULL TIME EMPLOYMENT	
71%	61%
COMMUNITY PARTICIPATION	
18%	8%
HOMEOWNERSHIP	
68%	52%
LIVING IN AN APARTMENT	
29%	63%
HOUSING CONDITIONS	
41% GOOD	49% GOOD
NEIGHBORHOOD CONDITIONS	
33% GOOD	32% GOOD
PRESENCE OF OFFICE USE IN THE NEIGHBORHOOD	
8%	11%
PRESENCE OF BUSINESSES USE IN THE NEIGHBORHOOD	
18%	20%
UNDERGRAD/COLLEGE EDUCATION ATTAINED	
28%	58%

Source: Based on the 2019 online survey by author.

Interestingly, the survey showed that educational attainment did increase across generations, coinciding with data from the Inter-American Development Bank; that, even though the region has low social mobility, educational mobility has improved.[5] This may demonstrate the exception that proves the rule: the fact that social mobility is low, even with higher education-attainment in relationship to the previous generation, indicates that the built environment is critical to allow an individual to move up the social ladder.

What Is Bogotá Doing to Fix It?

In 1974, the city deployed an event pilot called *Ciclovia* – the closure of major highways in Bogotá for residents to bike – which became a decree in 1976, making *Ciclovias* a permanent event every Sunday from 7:00 a.m. to 2:00 p.m. The event was meant to provide space for the community to bike, skate, run, or walk in a safe environment. This event was one of the first ones in the region to deliberately provide additional public open space for exercise and leisure. However, what is remarkable about this event is that it paved the way for a culture of the use of active mobility, not only as a means to exercise, but as way to mobilize people in their daily routine. *Ciclovias* evolved to *Ciclorrutas*, which are now permanent bike lanes where many residents commute to work or school providing an affordable mobility option for those without the means to purchase a car or pay for public transit (see Figure 2.3).

In 2013, a joint effort between the Secretary of Education and the Secretary of Mobility, created the *Al Colegio en Bici* (To School on a Bike) program to promote the use of the bicycle in the school-age population by lending bicycles and organizing daily biking tours between schools and neighborhood meeting points. The program includes *Cicloexpediciones* (Bikexpeditions) to cultural facilities and other parts of the city for children to know their neighborhoods, led by School Guides. According to the Secretary of Mobility, from 2013 to 2019, more than 15,000 low-income children benefited from this program. Bicycle lane coverage in the city has increased to 500 kilometers and construction work for the first metro line has begun (see Figure 2.4).

Figure 2.3 Bogotá Ciclo Ruta by Mark Pitt
Source: Shutterstock.

Figure 2.4 Bogotá Bike Lane Coverage by Camilo Espitia
Source: Based on information from Datos Abiertos Bogotá.

Some of the previously established goals from the early 2000s were the implementation of 431 kilometers of bicycle lanes, out of which 187 kilometers were built by 2018; 20 routes of Transmilenio (BRT), out of which nine were accomplished; 160 educational institutions, out of which 40 were built; and five cultural institutions, with one being built.

According to the 2019 Quality of Life Report by *Bogotá Como Vamos* (How Are We Doing, Bogotá?), in terms of education between 2015 and 2019, there were 12.55 percent less children out of the school system.

In terms of public space, there is a goal of 10 m^2 per habitant (6 m^2 for actual public space and 4 m^2 as green space) out of which 4.5 m^2 per habitant has been achieved.

In regards to housing, between 2012 and 2019, the city reached more than 9,000 settlements of legalizing and title paperwork.

However, one of the biggest endeavors the city is making to improve connectivity in the city is the drafting of the 2020–2024 POT, which aims to:

- Contribute to formal employment to reduce poverty with economic growth that does not compromise natural and social resources;
- Address socio-spatial segregation, also known as residential segregation that creates a geographic concentration of vulnerable housing, especially on the southern portion of the city;
- Understand the relationship between urban and the rural settings with development that affects land that was previously dedicated to agriculture, which compromises food security;
- Reduce congestion and commuting times that affect the quality of life and productivity through the implementation of sustainable public transit; and
- Include the surrounding municipalities in the planning efforts to coordinate shared natural, social, and economic resources.

There is work to do, as some of the goals have not been achieved in terms of infrastructure. However, what is noteworthy about this plan is the fact that it is comprehensive and looks beyond its borders as it understands Bogotá not as an isolated city but rather as a territory surrounded by several communities with which it has a symbiotic relationship in terms of resources and productivity, and this represents part of the social fabric that makes up the city.

The Future

Bogotá is in a unique period in its developmental history with this latest master plan and vigorous investment in public transportation. This is the opportunity to set its vision and discover the balance between development and social equity. It is an exceptional moment to build a city that is welcoming, diverse, and just – a city that provides the tools to navigate in all directions – including the socioeconomic ladder – to contribute to its own development and growth. The new plan is a mirror for the city to look at itself and see the difficulties as opportunities and celebrate those challenges as what makes the city unique. The city is building an environment that provides connectivity, safety, and health as part of Bogotá's efforts to improve equity in a way that is connected with its natural and cultural resources. The investment in transportation infrastructure, alternative modes of mobility, more green spaces, and an encouragement of mixed-use development has the potential to build a city with higher social mobility that is prosperous and environmentally resilient.

References

1 Alesina, A., Hohmann, S., Michalopoulos S. and Papaioannou, E. (2019) *Intergenerational Mobility in Africa*. National Bureau of Economic Research: Cambridge, MA.
2 Almandoz, A. (2002) *Planning Latin America's Capital Cities 1850–1950*. Routledge: London.
3 Angotti, T. (2017) *Urban Latin America: Inequalities and Neoliberal Reforms*. Rowman & Littlefield Publishers: Lanham.
4 Attia, A. (2005) Why should researchers report the confidence interval in modern research? *Middle East Fertility Society Journal* (Cairo), 10.
5 Azevedo, V. and Bouillon, C. (2009) *Intergenerational Social Mobility in Latin America: A Review of Existing Evidence*. Inter-American Development Bank: Washington, DC.
6 Bartlett, J. E., Kotrlik, J. W. and Higgins, C. C. (2001) Organizational research: Determining appropriate sample size in survey research. *Learning and Performance Journal*, 19, 43–50.
7 Benavides, M. (2017) *Una Mirada a La Gentrificación: El Caso Bogotá*. Colombian National University: Bogotá.
8 Bergman, M. M. (Ed.). (2008) *Advances in Mixed Methods Research: Theories and Applications*. Sage: Los Angeles.
9 Bernal, D. (2013) *School Desertion: A Problem of Social Character*. Santo Tomas University: Bogotá.
10 Blanden, J. and Machin, S. (2017) *Home Ownership and Social Mobility*. School of Economics, University of Surrey and Centre for Economic Performance, London School of Economics: London.
11 Bogota Mayor's Office. (2006) *Decree 449 of 2006 Bogota Educational Institutions Master Plan*. Bogota Mayor's Office: Government of Colombia.

12 Butler, S. and Cabello, M. (2018) *Housing as a Hub for Health, Community Services, and Upward Mobility*. The Brookings Institution: Washington, DC.
13 Camargo, A. and Hurtado, A. (2013) *Urbanización Informal en Bogotá: Agentes y Lógicas de Producción del Espacio Urbano*. Universidad Piloto de Colombia: Bogotá.
14 Cardeno, F. (2007) *History of the Urban Development of the Center of Bogota*. Bogotá Mayor's Office: Bogotá.
15 Castillo, C. and El Tiempo, D. (2019) *En Bogotá, hay 278.511 Venezolanos, Entre Regulares e Irregulares*. www.eltiempo.com/bogota/cuantos-venezolanos-hay-en-bogota-356600. Accessed February 15, 2021.
16 Chetty, R. Hendren, N. Kline, P. and Saez, E. (2014) *Where is the Land of Opportunity? The Geography of Intergenerational Mobility in the United States*. The Quarterly Journal of Economics: Oxford.
17 CIRT (Center for Innvoation in Reasearch and Teaching). *Overview of Mixed Methods*. Grand Canyon University Arizona. https://cirt.gcu.edu/research/developmentresources/research_ready/mixed_methods/overview. Accessed March 22, 2019.
18 Correa, J., et al. (2017) El tranvia de bogota, 1882–1951. *Revista de Economía Institucional*, 19(36).
19 Coutts, A. and Kawachi, I. (2006) The urban social environment and its effects on health. *Cities and the Health of the Public*, 49–60.
20 Creswell, J. (2009) *Research Design: Qualitative, Quantitative, and Mixed Methods Approaches* (3rd ed.). Sage: Los Angeles.
21 Creswell, J. and Clark, V. (2010) *Designing and Conducting Mixed Methods Research* (2nd ed.). Sage: Los Angeles.
22 Dalle, P. (2013) *Upward Social Mobility Trajectories of Families of Working Class Origin in the Metropolitan Area of Buenos Aires*. Núcleo Básico de Revistas Científicas Argentinas: Buenos Aires.
23 Davila, H. (2005) El Plan Maestro de Equipamientos Educativos en la Construcción de la Ciudad. *Bitácora Urbano Territorial*, 9(1), 27–42.
24 Doruk, O. Pastore, F. and Yavuz, H. (2019) *Low Social Mobility in Latin America May Hinder Economic Growth*. IZA World of Labor: Bonn.
25 Drakakis-Smith, D. (1986) *Urbanisation in the Developing World*. Routledge Library Editions: London.
26 Engelhardt, G., Eriksen, M., Gale, W. and Mills, G. (2010) What are the social benefits of homeownership? Experimental evidence for low-income households. *Journal of Urban Economics*, 67(3), 249–258.
27 Fahy, F. and Rau, H. (2013) *Methods of Sustainability Research in the Social Science*. (1st ed.). London: Sage.
28 Franco, R., Atria, R., and Leon, A. (2007) *Stratification and Social Mobility in Latin America*. Cepal. Washington, DC.
29 Galvis. and Meisel (2014) *Aspectos Regionales de la Movilidad Social y la Igualdad de Oportunidades en Colombia*. Banco de la República: Bogotá.
30 Galvis, L. (2012) *Informalidad Laboral en las Áreas Urbanas de Colombia*. Banco de la República: Bogotá.
31 Gilbert, A. (1998) *The Latin American City*. Latin American Bureau: London.
32 Gill, N. S. (2018) *The Walled Shang Dynasty Cities of Ancient China: The Capital Cities of the Historic Shang Emperors*. New York, NY. www.thoughtco.com/shang-dynasty-walled-cities-ancient-china-117664. Accessed June 27, 2019.

33 Grusky, D. and Cumberworth, E. (2010) *A National Protocol for Measuring Intergenerational Mobility*. Stanford Center for the Study of Poverty and Inequality: Stanford, CA.
34 Hernández, CE., Varela, L., Mena, V., Salamanca, O., Bright, P., Vanegas, D., Montaño, A., and Rojas, R. (2010) *Reflexiones Sobre Arquitectura y Ciudad*. Fundación Universidad de Bogotá Jorge Tadeo Lozano: Bogotá.
35 Kawachi, I. Kennedy, B. P. and Glass, R. (1999) Social capital and self-rated health: A contextual analysis. *American Journal of Public Health*, 89(8), 1187–1193.
36 Kendall, R. and Tulip, P. (2018) *The Effect of Zoning on Housing Prices*. Reserve Bank of Australia: Sydney.
37 Kothari, C. (2004) *Research Methodology: Methods and Techniques* (2nd ed.). New Delhi: New Age International.
38 Leitão, S. (2015) *Política de Mobilidade, Mercado de Terras e a Nova Lógica de Expansão na Curitiba Metrópole: Inclusão do Excluido?* Pontifícia Universidade Católica do Paraná: Pontifícia.
39 Ley 142 de 1994 Nivel Nacional.
40 Lubell, H. And McCallum, D. (1978) *Bogota: Urban Development and Employment*. International Labour Office: Geneva.
41 Marcel, M. (2009) *Movilidad, desigualdad, y política social en América Latina*. CEPLAN: Peru. https://www.cieplan.org/wp-content/uploads/2019/05/Paper-M_Marcel-Movilidad_Movilidad-desigualdad-y-pol-social-en-AL.pdf
42 Mazumdar, S., Learnihan, V., Cochrane, T. and Davey, R. (2017) *The Built Environment and Social Capital: A Systematic Review. Environment and Behaviour*. South Western Sydney Local Health District and University of Canberra: Liverpool.
43 Neidhöfer, G. Serrano, J. and Gasparini, L. (2017) *Educational Inequality and Intergenerational Mobility in Latin America: A New Database*. Univers idad Nacional de la Plata: La Plata.
44 Nina, E., Grillo, S. and Malaver, C. (2003) *Movilidad social y transmisión de la pobreza en Bogotá. Economía Y Desarrollo Vol. 2 Num. 2*. Universidad Autonoma de Colombia: Bogotá.
45 Nunn, A., Johnson, S., Monro, S., Bickerstaffe, T. and Kelsey, S. (2007) *Factors Influencing Social Mobility. Technical Report*. Her Majesty's Stationery Office and University of Huddersfield: Huddersfield.
46 Oishi, S., Koo, M. and Buttrick, N. R. (2019) The socioecological psychology of upward social mobility. *American Psychologist*, 74(7), 751–763.
47 Orozco, M., Espinosa, R., Fonseca, C., and Vélez, R. (2019) *The Informe de Movilidad Social en México 2019. Informa de Movilidad Social en Mexico 2019*. Centro de Estudios Espinosa Yglesias and Ciudad de Mexico: Mexico.
48 Piña, W. and Pardo, C. (2015) *Development and Urban Sustainability: An Analysis of Efficiency Using Data Envelopment Analysis*. Universidad del Rosario: Rosario.
49 Pla, J. and Rodríguez, J. (2016) *Tendencias de Movilidad Social en la Argentina de las dos Últimas Décadas: 1995–2010*. University of Buenos Aires and Social Sciences Faculty: Buenos Aires.
50 Portafolio. (2019) *Producto interno bruto de Bogotá supera al de tres países de la región*. www.portafolio.co/economia/producto-interno-bruto-de-bogota-supera-al-de-tres-paises-de-la-region-532324. Accessed November 11, 2020.
51 Ruiz, J. (2017) *Impactos sociales del proceso de gentrificación en barrios de origen informal. Caso de la localidad de Chapinero*. National University of Colombia: Bogotá.

52 Sale, J. E., Lohfeld, L. H. and Brazil, K. (2002) Revisiting the quantitative-qualitative debate: Implications for mixed-methods research. *Quality and Quantity*, 36(1), 43–53.
53 Sallis, J. F., Cerin, E., Conway, TL., Adams, MA., Frank, LD., Pratt, M., Salvo, D., Schipperijn, J., Smith, G., Cain, KL., Davey, R., Kerr, J., Lai, PC., Mitáš, J., Reis, R., Sarmiento, OL., Schofield, G., Troelsen, J., Van Dyck, D., De Bourdeaudhuij, I., and Owen, N. (2016) *Urban Environments in 14 Cities Worldwide Are Related to Physical Activity.* Lancet: London.
54 Saoud, R. (2002) *Introduction to the Islamic City.* FSTC Limited: London.
55 Secretary of Planning of Bogota. (2010) *Bogota, Ciudad de Estadisticas, Poblacion y Desarollo Urbano. Boletin 23.* Bogota Mayor's Office: Bogota.
56 Secretary of Planning of Bogota. (2013) *2013 Bogota Social Mobility Index Bulletin No. 58.* Bogotá Mayor's Office: Bogotá.
57 Sharkey, P. and Graham, B. (2013) *Mobility and the Metropolis. How Communities Factor Into Economic Mobility.* The PEW Chartable Trusts: Philadelphia.
58 Smolka, M. and Mullahy, L. (2007) *Perspectivas urbanas: Temas críticos en políticas de suelo en America Latina.* of Lincoln Institute Land Policy: Cambridge.
59 Talavera, H. (2005) *El plan maestro de equipamientos educativos en la construcción de la Ciudad.* Universidad Nacional de Colombia: Bogota.
60 Van Ham, M. Tammaru, T. de Vuijst, E. and Zwiers, M. (2016) *Spatial Segregation and Socio-Economic Mobility in European Cities.* Institute for the Study of Labor: Berlin.
61 Vargas, J., Goytia, C., Sanguinetti, P., Álvarez, A., Estrada, R., Brassiolo, P., Fajardo, G., and Daude, C. (2018) *Urban Growth and Access to Opportunities: A Challenge for Latin America.* Development Bank of Latin America: Venezuela.

3 Mexico City
Infrastructure and Water for All

– Today, 663 million people do not have access to improved water sources according to the World Health Organization.

September 19, 1985: An 8.1-magnitude earthquake shakes Mexico City, affecting mostly the areas with soft terrain composed of clay, killing and injuring thousands, and leaving, still today, an unknown number of unhoused people. After the earthquake, development in the city skyrocketed and new and larger buildings began populating the city, exacerbating the issue of water sources and aquifers and perpetuating the soil problems the city had endured for centuries. Since the earthquake, Mexico has modified its building codes to strict seismic-conditions construction requirements to avoid future damage. However, building codes alone do not solve these issues when development keeps spreading and adding pressure to the city's hydric and soil systems.

Exactly 32 years later, on the same date in 2017, another earthquake – this time of a magnitude of 7.1 – hit the city, causing yet another bulk of damage and victims. Earlier that month, I had been in Mexico participating in urban design projects in San Luis Potosí and Mexico City and became interested in the topic of water in Mexico. Site visits and conversations with experts and residents helped illustrate the issues that affect the city, not only with aquifers and soil composition, but the water supply more broadly to such an enormous city. Soil conditions in the city affected by the drainage of its underground water not only have an impact on the vulnerability to earthquakes and the soil's structural capacity but also on the water resources being depleted, and this reduces the access to clean water for many of its residents.[2, 6]

In this chapter, we will look at an overview of development in Mexico City and how it has affected its water resources. We will discuss the effects of the depletion of aquifers in the city and its effect on

DOI: 10.4324/9781003380818-3

the city's development, even after the building code enforcements after the 1985 earthquake; we will elaborate on the social, economic, and environmental benefits of improving these issues and examples of what Mexico City is already doing as part of its progress.

Water in Mexico City

Mexico City is one of the most important Latin American economies, home to 21 million people with a $20K USD a year GDP per capita.[22] Its prosperity and job opportunities attract millions every year. Similar to what was described in the Bogotá chapter, this population growth translates into uncontrolled development that further expands the city and adds pressure to its urban ecosystem. The increasing amount of developed land coverage jeopardizes the soil's filtration capacity while reducing its strength, its stability, and intensifying the risk of flooding. At the same time, the city's overdevelopment depletes clean water resources and deteriorates their quality.[18] With a population of over 20 million people, Mexico City raises concerns about its future development and the inability for many residents to access clean and affordable water.

The current circumstances include political, economic, social, technological, and environmental conversations that need to happen to mitigate the water shortage and flooding risks and to delineate a different trajectory for the future. Some of the strategies include infrastructure management to minimize waste, improvement of quality and service coverage, reduction of the pressure on the aquifers that supply the city, reduction of the risk of flooding, and improvement of infrastructure resiliency.

Background and Challenges

Located in a valley at 2,200 meters above sea level and close to the center of the country, the city was founded by the Mexica people in the year 1325 as the epicenter of the Aztec Empire under the name Tenochtitlan in the middle of what used to be Texcoco Lake.

Water has been an important infrastructure-management hurdle since its foundation. The Grand Tenochtitlan surrounded by the lake was gradually enlarged by the Aztecs by enveloping the island with artificial floating gardens called "*chinampas*." Tenochtitlan later became Mexico City under Spanish rule in 1521 and, by the time of colonization, the city had to be progressively drained to allow for expansion and to avoid flooding. In 1856, the Grand Channel was built to drain water out of the city due to massive inundations.

After severe flooding and contamination, a number of natural rivers were covered and enclosed, giving way to important vehicular roadways that now take the names of the rivers they cover.

Hiding the rivers in Mexico City has interfered with the natural water cycle that used these waterways as a drainage system. Trash dumped in the rivers flowed downstream, spreading pollution throughout the city, becoming a public health threat. In the second half of the twentieth century, the local government decided to tube and cover several of its rivers.[21, 27] After centuries of growth in the city, where waterways were progressively eliminated, riverbeds rerouted, and ground porosity decreased, flooding worsened. Graphic 3.1

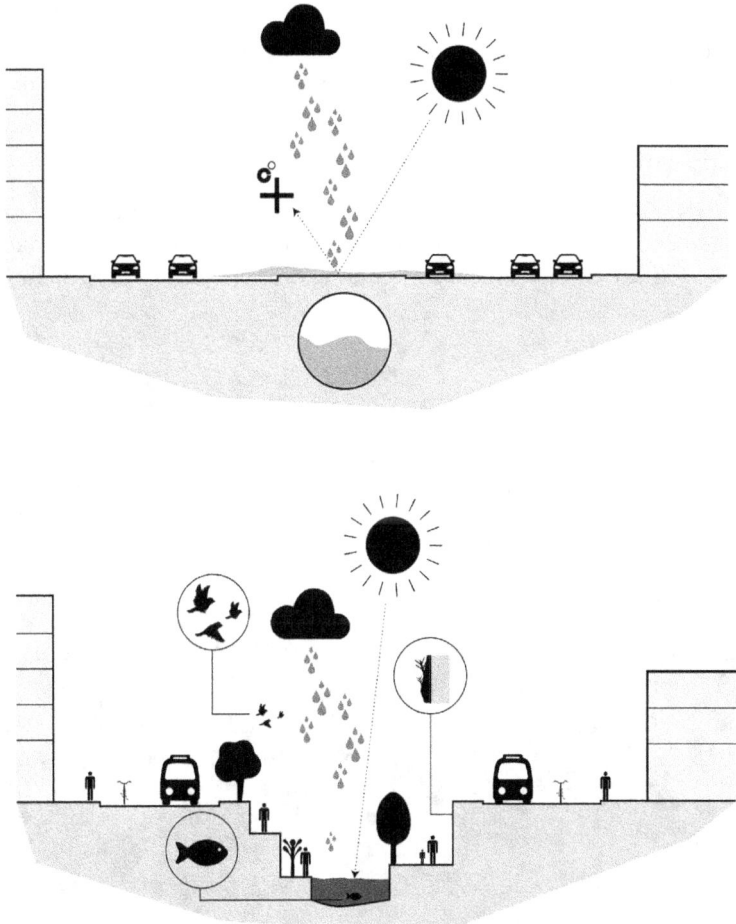

Figure 3.1 Reopening of City Canals by Camilo Espitia

shows the possibilities of reopening the canals while providing mobility in the city.

As of today, the city has not been able to entirely mitigate the risk of flooding, provide full potable water coverage, improve water quality and availability, and prevent the sinkage in parts of the city due to the depletion of aquifers. The Grand Channel, for example, has lost its natural slope due to soil subsiding and has become "counter-sloped," increasing flooding risk. The concerns about the water system's flexibility to expand, climate-change resiliency, and increased demand are yet to be addressed (see Figure 3.2).

Describing some of the different areas that define a city's operations helps to illustrate assets, opportunities, deficiencies, and risks to explain the complex scenarios that Mexico City faces with its water resources. A PESTEL analysis uncovers new approaches to reshape the system's current conditions (see Table 3.1).

Areas of Improvement

There are several measures that can help guide the supply and management of water in Mexico City. All of them are integrated in nature and require coordinated efforts among different disciplines, including

Figure 3.2 Sinking Street by Erlucho
Source: Shutterstock.

Table 3.1 **PESTEL** (Political, Economic, Social, Technological, Environmental, and Legal Implications in Planning) by Camilo Espitia

Political	Technological
In terms of planning, it refers to the community's leadership and support behind the implementation of planning strategies. It is critical for the political arm to work together with the qualified stakeholders to execute plans and acquire funding necessary for implementation. Water infrastructure planning and funding impact access equity.	In planning, this is referring to mapping tools such as GIS (Geographic Information Systems), sensors, and infrastructure in general. Outdated infrastructure prevents quality and quantity of water service to be provided evenly throughout the city. Understanding the existing infrastructural conditions, including location of sources, water lines, volumes, leaks, and flow is critical to a plan for sustainable water management system.
Economical	**Environmental**
Planning needs to incorporate both the initial and future costs of upgrading and maintaining infrastructure and also its funding sources. In terms of water in Mexico City, infrastructure investment, service fees, and maintenance are affected by the lack of an economic plan that considers the sustainable development of the city.	Planning needs to incorporate its natural resources in land-use development and the impact of such policies on those resources and the population as a means of environmental justice. Aquifers are being depleted due to increased demand. Uncontrolled development increases flooding risk, reduces the soil filtration capacity and aquifer replenishment, compromises the soil's structural capacity, and increases the heat-island effect.
Social	**Legal**
The social aspect of planning addresses the outcome of policies and their impact on the community and the input they can provide in producing strategies through public engagement and participation. It also includes the raising of awareness to inform and educate citizens on the management of resources. Outreach helps to understand the challenges of the community in terms of access to resources, while society's water habits are contributing to waste. An unequal access to services and waste exacerbates social inequalities in the city.	Planning includes the incorporation of the legal framework to monitor and enforce policies, including those that protect the environment, protect the people, and establish development rules with tools such as zoning and building codes. Policies need to be updated to regulate development, to control water usage, and to enforce accountability to manage water in the City.

the participation of the citizenry, to achieve sustainable development of Mexico City. Some of the measures include the reduction of water waste at distribution areas, control of consumer-usage waste, treatment and collection of water, adjustment of service pricing, control of the levels of ground porosity, planning for resiliency, reopening of several of the city's hydric systems that are currently closed to allow rainwater to naturally find its course within the ecosystem,[16] reinforcement of building code requirements for water storage and recycling units in buildings, and the control of the city's density by establishing a stronger interconnection with the Toluca as a satellite city.

Political (Policy and Planning Strategies)

The political will to implement policies or budgets takes longer than the usual public office term. Consequently, several plans to address issues with the water supply have been neglected. Strengthening the institutional sector would transform agencies in charge of infrastructure management into independent apolitical entities to enforce policy execution. Amapola Grijalva, an economist from National Autonomous University of Mexico, in the book *The Challenges in the Water Management in Mexico City*, expressed that the biggest challenge regarding Mexico City's water problem is political and social.[9]

For instance, Parque Ecológico Lago de Texcoco, a 12,000-hectare major green infrastructure project designed to collect water and reduce flooding, was interrupted in 2014 to make space for the New Mexico City International Airport as part of the presidential campaign winner at the time. Four years, millions of dollars, and several social protests later, construction work for the airport was interrupted by the new government to resume the construction of the ecological park. Political goals need to be designed as part of the sustainable-planning process to avoid disparate objectives and incongruent decisions.[7]

Density could be decompressed by leveraging satellite surrounding-communities. Located 63 kilometers from Mexico City and bearing economic importance in the area, the city of Toluca offers an opportunity to establish an administrative interconnection to alleviate the pressure of population growth. According to Jody Milder in the book *Sustainable Urban Environment*, satellite cities are smaller independent cities connected to a larger city through the enlargement of their footprint.[25] Because an actual physical connection is imperative for the relationship to work, a high-speed rail system is being built to connect both cities. This means that a regional planning strategy that considers Mexico City as a collection of communities outside its administrative boundaries is key to managing its resources.

Additionally, citizen participation is essential to find solutions. Their awareness of the problem and willingness to participate is an opportunity to improve and expedite policies to access sustainable water services and to demand accountability and transparency. Citizenry participation also contributes to real-time reporting of infrastructure issues such as leakage, flooding, or water quality. In 2003, the Mexico City Water Systems Agency (SACMEX) was created to take over the operations of drinking water, sewage, and water treatment in the city. This autonomous entity enjoys a flexibility that allows it to more quickly and efficiently execute policies independent of the central local government while allowing citizens to request transparency reports for greater accountability.

Economic Factors (Investment and Pricing)

Several economic issues are interconnected with the management of the water infrastructure in Mexico City. The foremost challenge in terms of technology and infrastructure is the financing and investment to update aging systems in the network. Nations with financial challenges use tools such as PPIs[10] (private participation in infrastructure) as financing strategies to invest in infrastructure that can come from sources that allow for private foreign investment.[28] Even though Mexico is not part of the eligible countries to receive IDA (International Development Association) resources from the World Bank, PPIs help to increase a government's credibility in the eyes of the private sector, other governments, and the citizenry. This must be done within a strong political framework to avoid the impact on costs when the private sector responds to market trends.

The second item (and inherently connected to the social aspect of service accessibility) is the pricing of water. The service pricing needs to shift to a system where the poorer sector of the population can afford the services for a price according to their income. In Colombia, for example, as described in the Bogotá chapter, the higher-value property owners pay a premium on all utilities to help subsidize those with lower value properties. A fixed price can be an obstacle for the majority of the citizens, therefore increasing an inequality gap that is not acceptable in a sustainable, just city.[14]

The third item is productivity, which can be affected by losses and damages to property and by the interruption on the normal functions of the city by environmental disasters, including water-related catastrophes. With a $20K USD a year GDP per capita,[22] if the city were to interrupt its daily functions due to major flooding, its loses would amount to billions of dollars. Resiliency strategies need to be a part of the management system to accommodate and protect assets during unforeseen events.

Social (Education – Equality of Access)

According to the World Health Organization (WHO), an individual needs between 50 and 100 liters of water per day to meet basic needs and protect their health. The Consultive Water Council of Mexico published that, in 2017, Mexico City reached a consumption of 360 liters of water per person per day[20] compared to 170 liters in Santiago de Chile.[17] This is between three and a half to seven times the average needed amount.

Mexico City loses 40 percent of its water due to leaks in its network,[1] not counting the waste after it leaves the system and enters the buildings. This is more than the total 35 percent of water waste in Bogotá.[8] This makes Mexico City one of the Latin American capitals that consumes and wastes water in higher volumes.

A disproportionate access to water in this megacity intensifies the inequalities already present. A market-driven pricing system causes sectors of the population to have shortages of water. Furthermore, the east side of the city has more water-supply challenges because the main sources (Lerma and Cutzamala) are located west of the national capital.

Inequality in service access creates a social burden that needs to improve by putting emphasis on the geographic location of water-collection systems and treatment plants and by establishing a new pricing system (explained later in this chapter) to guarantee equal access to water, including resilient policies that help respond to natural disasters. For example, after the 2017 earthquake, the eastern part of the city, including the Tláhuac, Iztapalapa, and Xochimilco districts, suffered an interruption of water service due to leakage on the system, which confirmed the inequalities in water access in Mexico City.[3]

However, that same year, the local government of Mexico City approved the Water and Hydric Sustainability Law. This document proposed the creation of a Consulting Council that would include the academic sector, NGOs, and the private sector to allow public participation and contribute to shaping policies and making decisions on the future of water in the city.

Technological (Infrastructure and Smart Technologies)

The aging infrastructure that contributes to water waste adds pressure to the hydric sources of the city. Since the average supply of water is 32.7m3/s out of which 22.4m3/s comes from aquifers and 9.5m3/s from the Cutzamala River, the city's aquifers are at risk of being overused and their capacity compromised.[20] Because those aquifers refill at a slower rate than the extraction, it causes soil's subsidence (see Figure 3.3).

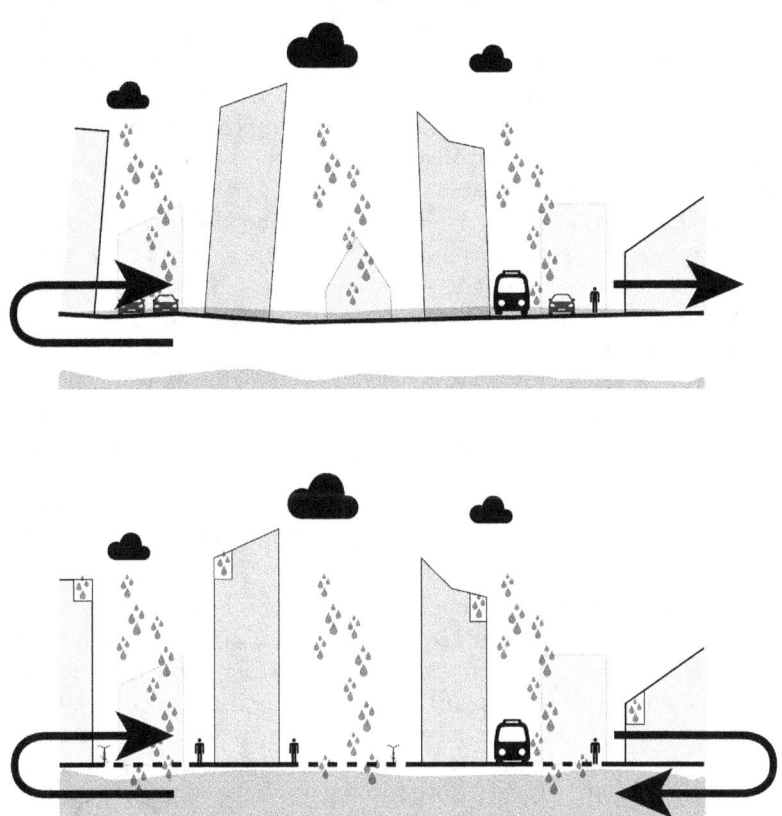

Figure 3.3 Ground Porosity in Mexico City by Camilo Espitia

The overexploitation of the aquifers also reduces the flow volume of rivers that feed from them forcing deeper excavations to find water. This increases construction costs and lowers the water quality due to the exposure of more underground particles.

The Cutzamala system provides 23.7 percent of potable water in both Mexico City and Toluca[5] and, after four decades of service, is already experiencing the pressures of the city's growth, population increase, and the agricultural and environmental practices that jeopardize its integrity. This system needs to be accommodated to respond to the city's current and future growth.

This system and its relationship with Mexico City's geological challenges is critical to the supply of water of many of its residents. Although after the September 2017 earthquake there were no damages to the system and only temporary brown water sedimentation was seen in parts of the city,[19] in June 2020, after a smaller seismic movement, the system did suffer damages that interrupted services for several days.[11]

Technology can be introduced into new mechanical and plumbing code requirements for all buildings such as efficient plumbing fixtures, leakage sensors, and water storage and recycling units for self-sufficiency toward water demands. Building codes could require smart metering applications for users to understand and raise awareness on their water-use practices to modulate wasteful behavior and to understand the impact of their water habits. Options of passive technologies for water storage and recycling also need to be intrinsic to the urban ecosystem. In 2019, the National Water Commission (Conagua) created the MAPAS (Drinking Water, Sewage, and Treatment Manual), a set of design guidelines for water, sewage, and treatment-plant recommendations, which, although thorough, was not intended to be a set of requirements. Technology such as leakage sensors could also be incorporated into the system to monitor inefficiencies because there is both visible and non-visible leakage.

Investing in technology can contribute to a resilient system that can more easily prepare for future expected (i.e., population increase) events and unexpected ones (i.e., storm, severe leakage). It can contribute to developing plans that can tackle issues such as lack of potable water, flooding, waste-water flooding, water contamination, or lack of water-source backup to ensure an uninterrupted service to all residents in the city. Improving the water management system in Mexico City improves livability, makes it easier to adjust to population growth and other threats, reduces health risks, controls and prevents transmittable disease, and improves social equilibrium by means of equal access to basic services in the city.

What Is Being Done?

The impetus of the city's government to improve the quality of service and increase the coverage or potable water throughout the city is strong. Claudia Sheinbaum, Mexico City's current mayor, plans to build treatment plants to use water from different sources to expand the availability of water. At the same time, nonprofits and NGOs such as the Fondos de Agua in Mexico City are implementing the Cosecha Capital (Capital Harvest) program to increase rainwater collection in the city.

The Parque Hídrico La Quebradora is a sustainable urban intervention that uses an abandoned plot of land located in a low-income part

Figure 3.4 Parque Hídrico La Quebradora by Municipalidad de la Ciudad de México

of the city. The site is a public park and a water collection system that helps mitigate flooding, reduces the temperature around the area, provides green spaces, cleans the air, and supplies clean water for the surrounding community.[4] This development is an example of interdisciplinary design and public-private partnerships.[15]

Located in the Iztapalapa delegation, Quebradora Park demonstrates how the built form addresses social resiliency[24] (see Figure 3.4). It does so by evolving with its context and letting the context drive social change in a community with a combination of green infrastructure and public space. Most of the water resources and treatment plants that feed Mexico City come from the west of the urban footprint, and by the time they get to that area of the city, because of failing infrastructure, either the water pressure is very low, or often, there is simply no potable water available. Moreover, because of overdevelopment and the amount of asphalt spread out throughout the city, when it rains, the area floods because rain cannot percolate through the ground. Due to overdevelopment, there is little open green space for the residents in that borough.

The designers of this 3.84-ha park opened up the ground to allow water to filter through, collect water to provide for the adjacent residents, reduce the risk of flooding, and provide open green spaces for the community. The park includes features such as water tanks, water filtration systems, cisterns, solar panels, vertical urban gardens, public transportation, bicycle amenities, a cafeteria, retail spaces, an auditorium, a skate park, a running track, soccer fields, picnic areas, sidewalks, children's playgrounds, a gym, and a viewing platform as part of its program. This hydric infrastructure project responds to the existing conditions and becomes part of the natural and social fabric in this part of the city, flexing between a plaza or a pond, as needed.

In 2016, concerned with the impact of development on woodlands and agricultural land on the outskirts of the city, the Secretariat of the Environment of Mexico City (SEDEMA) and the National Commission for the Knowledge and Use of Biodiversity (CONABIO) released a study called Biodiversity in Mexico City. This study helps define strategies for the conservation and sustainable use of the biodiversity in the city, which includes its natural resources, climate, and geology.[23]

In 2014, the city began the construction of the *Tren Interurbano*, an elevated, 57.7-km rail connecting Mexico City and Toluca as part of the National Development Plan 2013–2018 as a way to reduce carbon emissions, generate employment, decrease vehicular traffic and accidents, and provide additional mobility options to the community. The line is expected to start operations in 2023.

In April of 2019, Mexico City implemented a rainwater-collection program to improve water access in low-income areas and those with limited access to potable water. It consisted of the installation of water-collection tanks aimed at 10,000 households. The program began in the Iztapalapa and Xochimilco areas and includes the training of the community to operate and maintain the system.[12]

Mexico City's mayor also implemented the Hydrometric Sectorization, which consists of dividing the network into sectors, which helps to control leaks in the service, make the system more efficient, and ensure access to the entire city. By 2021, 265 of the 830 sectors had technology that detects leaks, measures the flows and pressure, and helps prioritize repairs.[13]

Also, in 2019, the city began the "No La Riegues" (Do Not Irrigate it or, colloquially, Do Not Mess It Up) campaign to raise awareness of waste and to promote conscientious behavior toward the use of water. In March of the same year, 150 technical support teams were introduced to detect and repair leaks in the system operating 24 hours a day.

The previous examples depict the success of the private and public sectors working together to address water scarcity.

Mexico City Tomorrow

Given the size of the challenge of water management in Mexico City, it is evident that there is no single solution to this problem. A number of components, including technology, diverse stakeholders, funding, education, infrastructure, and other policies need to convert water consumption into a fair and just closed-loop system that replenishes sources, reduces waste, and covers the entire city.[16] Water is a limited source, after all, and to make it "infinite," waste needs to be eliminated and water collection, recycling, and source replenishment need to be part of the system.[26] However, the challenge is not only technological or economic. Social changes are also necessary for citizens to be more judicious about consumption habits and the amount of water and purposes for which it is being used while the public sector and elected officials needs to keep the focus directed toward a smart, sustainable Mexico City.

Mexico City was born in water and protecting its waters is its future. There is an opportunity to see water as a symbol of its origins and a beacon of its destiny. For Mexico City, water is life. Water is health. Water is wellbeing. And, in its urban context, water is the path to justice and social equity.

References

1 Aristegui Noticias. (2019) *Se desperdicia 40% de agua por fugas en la CdMx: Sacmex.* https://agua.org.mx/se-desperdicia-40-de-agua-por-fugas-en-la-cdmx-sacmex-aristegui-noticias-2/. Accessed August 14, 2020.
2 Arreola, J. (2012) *Ingeniería de Resiliencia Aplicada para la Disminución de la Vulnerabilidad en el Sistema Hidráulico de la Ciudad de México.* (1st ed.). Javier Arreola Rosales: Mexico.
3 Asamblea Legislativa del Distrito Federal. (2017) *Medalla Merito Ciudadano Gaceta Parlamentaria/*. Accessed April 25, 2017.
4 Capital 21 Canal. (2018) *Conoce dónde será el parque Hídrico La Quebradora.* [Online Video], 29 January 2018. www.youtube.com/watch?v=M2_Ye5yqu64. Accessed August 4, 2018.
5 CONAGUA. (2017) *Presas y Acueductos Para Abastecimiento de Agua Potable.* Secretaria del Medio Ambiente: Mexico City.
6 Delgado-Ramos, G. (2015) Water and the political ecology of urban metabolism. *The Case of Mexico City,* 22(17).
7 Delgado, A. (2016) *El Nuevo Aeropuerto "inconstitucional, muy costoso y de altísimo riesgo".* www.proceso.com.mx/nacional/2016/1/28/el-nuevo-aeropuerto-inconstitucional-muy-costoso-de-altisimo-riesgo-158414.html. Accessed September 23, 2019.

8. Departamento Nacional de Planeacion. (2015) *En La Guajira se pierde el 82% del agua potable.* www.dnp.gov.co/Paginas/En-LaGuajira-se-pierde-el-82-del-agua-potable-.aspx. Accessed June 3, 2017.
9. Dominguez, R., Grijalva, A., Guasch, JC., Hernández, F., Ponce, J., and Rodarte, L. (2006) *Los retos de la gestión del agua en la Ciudad de México.* Fundación Heberto Castillo Martínez A.C: Mexico City.
10. Fu, T. Chen, H. and Choi, Y. (2016) Does the sustainable PPI investments. *Promote Financial Market's Sustainable Development?* 1(18).
11. Gabby, L. (2020) Daños en sistema Cutzamala por el sismo, afecta suministro de agua en Edomex. www.aquien.mx/danos-en-sistema-cutzamala-por-el-sismo-afecta-suministro-de-agua-en-edomex/. Accessed December 19, 2020.
12. Gobierno de la Ciudad de Mexico. (2020) Gaceta oficial la ciudad de méxico de. *Secretaria del Medio Ambiente del Gobierno de la Ciudad de México*, 267.
13. Gobierno de la Ciudad de Mexico. (2021) *Registra Gobierno capitalino avance de casi 35 por ciento en sectorización de agua en la Ciudad de México.* https://www.jefaturadegobierno.cdmx.gob.mx/comunicacion/nota/registra-gobierno-capitalino-avance-de-casi-35-por-ciento-en-sectorizacion-de-agua-en-la-ciudad-de-mexico#:~:text=En%20el%20marco%20del%20D%C3%ADa,fugas%2C%20realizar%20la%20medici%C3%B3n%20de. Mayor's Office.
14. Instituto Nacional de Estadística y Geografía. (2015) *Panorama Sociodemografico de Ciudad de Mexico 2015.* INEGI 51: Mexico City.
15. Lafarge Holcim Foundation. (2018) *Hydropuncture in Mexico.* www.lafarge-holcim-foundation.org/projects/hydropuncture. Accessed July 29, 2018.
16. Monroy, O. (2017) *Manejo sustentable de recursos para la Ciudad de México desde una visión de cuenca. Ponencia Presentada en el Marco del Foro de Trabajo: Consensos Para la Construcción de la Nueva ley de aguas y la Contraloría Ciudadana para la Ciudad de México, Casa de la Paz.* Universidad Autónoma Metropolitana: Metropolitana.
17. Ortiz, J. (2016) *Agua: Yo Consumo, Tu Consumes, Ellos Consumen, Todos Derrochamos?.* www.cedeus.cl/agua-yo-consumo-tu-consumes-ellos-consumen-todos-derrochamos/. Accessed March 14, 2022.
18. Peralta, J. (1982) El uso del agua en la ciudad de México. *Ciencias núm. 2, julio-agosto*, 42–53.
19. Rivera, A. (2017) *Sismo enturbia el agua del Sistema Cutzamala.* www.milenio.com/estados/sismo-enturbia-el-agua-del-sistema-cutzamala. Accessed April 15, 2019.
20. SACMEX. (2007) Hacia una gestión integral y sustentable del agua. *El reto: Primero el Agua*, 1(16).
21. Sanchez, A. (2016) *Los ríos invisibles de la Ciudad de México.* www.univision.com. www.univision.com/noticias/citylab-medio-ambiente/los-rios-invisibles-de-la-ciudad-de-mexico. Accessed July 12, 2018.
22. SEDECO. (2021) *Mexico City is Among the Largest and Best Performing Economies in the Americas.* Gobierno de la Ciudad de Mexico. Mexico City, Mexico.
23. SEDEMA. (2015) *Biodiversdad CDMX.* http://data.sedema.cdmx.gob.mx/biodiversidadcdmx/fauna.html. Accessed July 21, 2018.
24. Taller Capital. (2018) *Arquitectura, Construcción y Desarrollo Mobiliario.* www.tallercapital.mx. Accessed August 8, 2018.

25 Valdelamar, J. (2017) *México, el quinto país que más consume agua.* www.elfinanciero.com.mx/economia/mexico-el-quinto-pais-que-mas-consume-agua. Accessed August 20, 2018.
26 van Bueren, E. van Bohemen, H., Itard, L., and Visscher, H. (2011) *Sustainable Urban Environments: An Ecosystem Approach.* (1st ed.). Springer Science & Business Media: Dordrecht.
27 Villasana, C. and Gomez, R. (2017) *Los ríos de la ciudad que hoy ya no vemos.* www.eluniversalunivision.com.mx. www.eluniversal.com.mx/entrada-de-opinion/colaboracion/mochilazo-en-el-tiempo/nacion/sociedad/2017/06/21/los-rios-de-la. Accessed August 12, 2018.
28 World Bank. (2018) Investments in IDA Countries. *Private Participation in Infrastructure* (PPI), 1(24).

4 Lima

Air Quality and Environmental Justice

The week before Christmas in 1996, an explosion opened a hole in the wall of the Japanese Embassy in Lima during a celebration of Emperor Akihito's birthday, hosted by Morihisa Aoki, ambassador of Japan in Peru. Fourteen members of the Túpac Amaru Revolutionary Movement (MRTA) entered the building and held several hostages, making a series of demands to the government, then led by President Alberto Fujimori, that included the liberation of MRTA prisoners captured during the war against terrorism in the country. After several failed negotiations and four months and six days, in April 22, 1997, the government launched a rescue operation with 140 special-operations Peruvian squad-members that liberated all but one of the hostages and represented the end of the MRTA and a victory against terrorism.

Before that, on September 12, 1992, Abimael Guzman, the leader of the "Sendero Luminoso" (Shining Path), a guerrilla faction born in the late 1960s that committed its first violent attack in 1980, was arrested and put on trial. Twelve days later, in a black-and-white striped suit and inside a cage-like outdoor prison, Guzman's images went around the globe when he was presented to the press on the patio of a government building in Lima. Since the late 1960s and for almost three decades, the country experienced a period of relentless violence whose victims were mostly the population in the countryside. The collateral damage of this war cost thousands of lives, including the rural population that coercively migrated to Lima, escaping the cruelty of the revolutionary groups and the anti-terrorist groups on the state side fighting them. This civil battle, similar to the internal conflict in Colombia that lasted for decades, in addition to corruption, had had a negative effect on the economy of the country.

In 1990, Peru began moving toward an economic aperture that would propel the economy after years of social and political instability.

DOI: 10.4324/9781003380818-4

With the goal of reintroducing the Peruvian economy onto the world stage, market liberalization and deregulation policies lowered inflation and increased Peru's GDP. The country of Lima entered into a recovery period that brought with it an increase in consumption habits, migration patterns, and economic development. Similar to what occurred in other capitals in Latin America, the residential demand grew and the available, affordable land in Lima moved toward the periphery, demanding the expansion of services such as transportation, electricity, waste disposal, water, and sewage.

The balance between growth, development, and the preservation of the environment is one of many internal battles in the identity of cities. Lima is, and has been, like most city capitals in Latin America, the most important economic center of Peru throughout its history. Its development is key, not only to the residents of Lima, but to Peruvians as a whole.[18] As more and more people keep looking at the capital as the center of opportunities, it is imperative to make sure the city can adapt to these changes and provide quality of life for its citizens.

In this chapter, we will look at an overview of the development of Lima and how it has affected its natural resources, including its air quality. I will explain the effects of the low air-quality indicators in the city; I will then elaborate on the importance of improving these issues and will provide examples of what Lima can improve and what it has done so far to mitigate the impact of development on its air quality.

Background

The capital of Peru is located at the center of the country's coast, flanked by the Pacific Ocean to the west and the continental mountain range of the Andes to the east. The Callao area (part of metropolitan Lima) is a natural harbor deemed as the most important port in the country. Abundant wetlands are home to rich fauna and flora and several mountains give birth to numerous streams that are the sources of water for the city, including the Rimac River, from which the city acquired its name.

Comparable to the foundation of Mexico City on existing native settlements, Lima was founded by Spanish conquistador Francisco Pizarro in 1535 on land that belonged to the Inca Empire and that was occupied by earlier communities that had built canals to make the land more suitable for crops before the arrival of the Incas in 1470.

The city quickly became the most important metropolis in the viceroyalty of Spain and the most well-known city in South America, representing the political power of the Spanish crown in the Americas. The central plaza, today named Plaza de Armas, was located deliberately near the edge of the river to control the water distribution through canals that were built and maintained by the pre-Columbian communities of the Inca Empire, which was a defining factor in the land-use structure and development of Lima going forward.

The canals that once took water to communities and territories that were part of the Inca Empire were slowly replaced by development after the Spanish colonization, and the effect is evident on the geography of Lima and its drier conditions and loss of agricultural land. These green fields relied on the river and its canals for food production and vegetation due to the city's climate and geographic conditions that for the most part did not produce rain.

During the growth of the city throughout the sixteenth century, a series of canals was built to provide water for additional development, and with this came the challenges of water contamination. For public health reasons, city officials covered the canals and began extracting groundwater to replace the service. The Spanish crown around this time was still in the process of testing water, sanitation, and hygiene methods. These experiments were still part of a learning curve in Madrid (which had become the home of the court in 1561) and in other New World colonies, and it was not only until 1856 that the Spanish capital achieved the breakthrough of the Canal de Isabel II, with a new sewage network with improved design criteria.[38] Unfortunately for Lima, the excess manipulation of water sources and population growth depleted the city of water and made it the second-largest city in the world to be in a desert, only after Cairo.

Between 1684 and 1687, walls were built around the perimeter to protect what was known as the "City of Kings" from external attacks, only to be later removed in 1868 to respond to the increasing population. In 1881, during the War of the Pacific between Chile and a coalition between Bolivia and Peru, Lima was occupied by Chilean forces and several parts of the city were destroyed; however, the cultural and social damages were also part of the destruction of the development of Lima. During the occupation, the population remained inside their homes unless essential tasks required them to go into the streets.

The end of the nineteenth century and the first decades of the twentieth century brought a national reconstruction period after the war, which coincided with a growing demand for products from Europe that helped the Peruvian economy grow. Lima went through an urbanization period that brought the tramway in 1906 and the creation of periphery settlements to decompress what was considered the overpopulated center of the city.

By the mid-twentieth century, Lima had expanded beyond the demolished walls and saw its periphery grow farther out due to growing immigration from the countryside. This process began in the 1940s; however, that began to be reflected in its urban form by the 1950s. New settlements, known as "Pueblos Jovenes" (Young Towns), were slums that started populating the city and triggered the expansion of infrastructure such as electricity by community groups that organized financial structures to afford these services. The 1980s brought an economic crisis that made the socioeconomic differences in the city more evident.

Today, after years of migration into the city and an urbanization process that has forged social inequity and high contamination levels, Lima is on the verge of becoming a megacity. With a population of more than nine million, Lima is the fifth most populated city in Latin America and one of the 30 most populated cities in the world.[20]

Natural Environment, Quality of Life, and Economic Development

Arguably, there are endless attributes that define "quality of life." The World Health Organization defines "quality of life" through the lens of the context of an individual's culture and values. Nevertheless, the relationship with the natural environment affects the citizens' quality of life, while natural resources are essential economically.[45] From an urban-planning point of view, natural resources, open space, air quality, and mobility contribute to quality of life, while economic development without consideration of natural resources has the potential to affect it negatively.

Lima's industrial and transportation sectors have disparate effects on the life of some of its residents. While they are essential to Lima's economy, their impact on the air can lead to a number of diseases that include headaches, stress, fatigue, respiratory diseases, mental health issues, and cancer.

How do you balance quality of life and economic prosperity? How do you encourage progress without threatening natural resources? The emphasis of this chapter is on urban infrastructure, such as green open space, transportation, waste management, and land use planning, because those are the mechanisms that planners employ to have a positive impact on the quality of air of a city. The lack of planning for those systems results in environmental injustice today and for future generations.[39] While economic development depends on factors beyond urban planning and is related to strategies that may trickle down from a national economic agenda, it is possible to plan for local strategies that promote economic prosperity in parallel with policies that protect the natural and social resources of a community.[3]

Lima's Economy and Land Uses

Lima is the economic engine of Peru, representing almost half of the GDP of the entire country. Because of its qualified workforce, Lima concentrates more than half of the industrial production and almost half of the formal enterprising of the country. There is, however, a flip side to the productivity strength of the city and the centralist economic and administrative policies of Peru.

With 45 percent of the total enterprise in Lima dedicated to the sales and repairs of vehicles and motorcycles and an industrial production that includes textiles, metalworking, and the processing of food and beverages,[19] the city's natural resources are under threat, including its very own air quality. According to the World Health Organization, Lima is the most contaminated city in Latin America,[48] and more than 15,000 Peruvians die due to respiratory and cardiac diseases every year.[13] Diversifying the strength of the economy of the city and the country is critical to reducing the pressure on the city and its impact on the national economy. Lima's service and commerce sectors could benefit from a multi-node approach taking advantage of the already-established South, North, and East districts as established in its "2040 Diagnosis of the Productivity and Economic Synthesis" by the Metropolitan Planning Institute of Lima. This means that investing in development strategies that highlight these areas as strong, walkable cores of the city can reduce car dependency and mitigate the inequalities of air pollution in certain areas of Lima (as will be explained later). They also have the potential to become employment centers that provide economic opportunities for its residents already living in those areas so they need not commute for long times to access jobs. Strengthening the service and commerce economic sectors can further reduce the dependency on the industrial sector that is a burden on the city's natural resources.

Green Spaces

Lima is on the lower spectrum of urban green space per capita in the Latin American region. The Peruvian National System of Environmental Information (SINIA in Spanish) established that the city has an average of 4.82 m^2/habitant compared to the 15.1 m^2/habitant in Mexico City, 6 m^2/habitant in Buenos Aires,[9] and 6.30 m^2/habitant in Bogotá.[8]

Table 4.1 by Camilo Espitia, From Information by the National System of Environmental Information from the Secretary of Environment of Peru

Urban Green Area Per Inhabitant in Metropolitan Lima	
District	Area m^2
San Isidro	22.09
Miraflores	13.84
Pachacamac	0.85
Villa Maria del Triunfo	0.37
Pucusana	0.11

However, while the wealthiest districts of San Isidro and Miraflores have 22 and 13 square meters of green space per habitant respectively, districts such as Pucusana, Pachacamac and Villa Maria del Triunfo, do not even reach one square meter per resident (see Table 4.1).[44]

Trees and green areas not only absorb CO2; they also help control temperature and help provide oxygen, contributing to the air quality, especially in urban settings. What is more concerning about these numbers is that the collection of data does not take into consideration private green spaces, which may mean the gaps might be greater in the wealthiest neighborhoods.

Waste Management

Waste management in Lima is detrimental to its air quality. In 2016, the city produced more than 8,000 tons of waste a day,[7] and according to the campaign "Together for the Environment" (Juntos por el Medio Ambiente), only about 1 percent of waste was recycled. Some of the challenges in waste management in Lima are found in the informality with which waste is handled without consideration of adequate technical, sanitary, or environmental concerns.

Some of the issues with the way waste is handled in Lima include the handling and separation in unsuitable locations and poor conditions, generating health risks for the recyclers and their surroundings; the transportation of waste in unsuitable vehicles and equipment on public roads; the disposal of waste in inappropriate locations close to schools, community centers, or farming areas;[32] the lack of citizenry education and awareness of adequate waste disposal and opportunities; and the shortage of trash disposals areas in Lima with only three landfill locations with a total of 749.4 ha and only one plant for waste transferring and separation.

Traffic

According to the El Comercio survey, when asked about pollution caused by traffic, 90 percent of residents in Lima think most of the contamination is produced by buses and *combis* (minibuses), while only 2 percent think it caused by the use of private vehicles.[6] However, it is private vehicles that contaminate the most from the transportation sector,[25] which, added to industrial emissions, acid rain, heating and cooling systems from fossil fuels, inadequate waste disposal, and lack of green areas and arborization, makes Lima the city with the worst air quality in the region,[25] affecting the health of the most vulnerable of the population.

The vehicular sector produces between 70 percent and 80 percent of the polluting emissions in Lima's air.[37] And it is not difficult to see how heavy traffic in the city can take a high environmental toll on Lima. During my visit to Lima in 2018 on my way from the airport to the hotel, a 20-kilometer trip took about an hour and a half. Air pollution is a detrimental feature in the life of Limeños.

When checking the World Air Quality Index for the real-time air-quality conditions of different areas of Lima on October 20, 2022, the air quality index for San Juan de Lurigancho was 162, which is categorized as harmful for sensitive groups, such as children and people with respiratory diseases – higher than Metro Estrella Station in Medellin at 89, and much higher than the Acumar Station in Buenos Aires at 46 at exactly the same date and time.[50]

For decades, the transportation system in Lima has been defined by its informality. Free-market strategies from the decades of the 1990s opened up the transportation sector in Lima in favor of increasing the coverage in the city, causing overpopulation of vehicles legally providing public transportation services. Replacing them means carrying the risk of not covering the demand with any new implemented system. The saturation of the infamous "combis" (small and mid-size buses) is hazardous and hinders traffic flows. In Lima there are currently about 31,000 "combis"[40] and more than 200,000 taxis (see Figure 4.1).[4] The inconvenience of the system has encouraged the use of private vehicles, which worsens congestion on the roads.

To mitigate the problem, the city has implemented the metro and the BRT system. However, while these services cover the entire city, "combis" are still a major form of transportation for most of the residents. Although conventional public transportation caused 40 percent of fatalities in 2018,[12] and it is one of the main causes of traffic congestion in Lima, "combis" are still a convenient transportation

Figure 4.1 Combis in Lima by Camilo Espitia

mode for citizens with limited resources because they have lower prices and cover smaller areas in remote neighborhoods. However, in the entire country, issues such as traffic congestion, the higher costs of different modes, or the detriment to the environment generate US$20 billion in losses a year.[41]

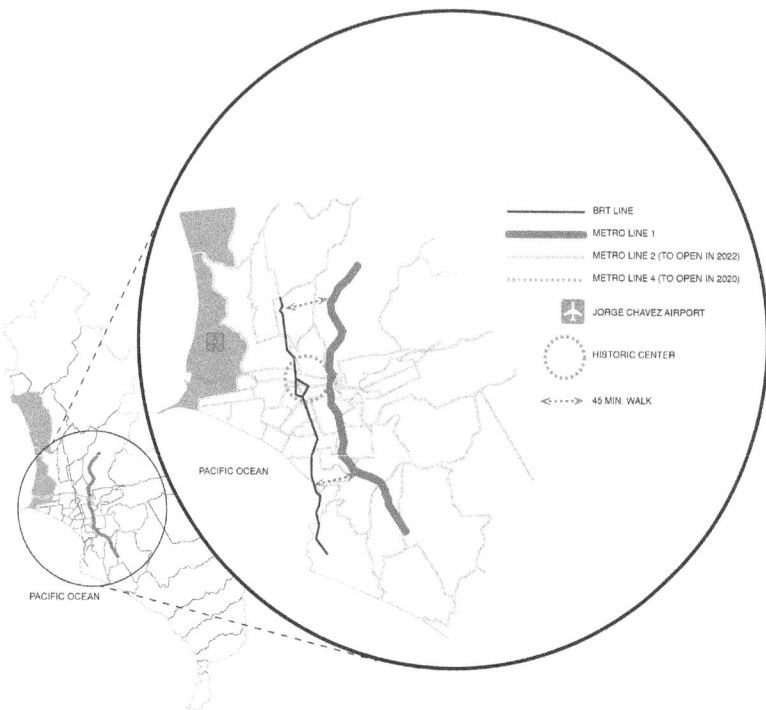

Figure 4.2 Transportation Coverage by Camilo Espitia

The city has added bicycle lanes to its network as alternative modes of transportation to alleviate traffic and reduce pollution with a total of 141 kilometers of bike lanes as of 2017, compared to the 392 kilometers in Bogotá, the highest in the region (see Figure 4.2).[42] In fact, some of the implementation in Lima's bicycle network has used Bogotá as a reference.[35, 46] Walking is still an option, although in many parts of the city, the culture of the car prevails, endangering pedestrians.

Yet another issue is the temperature inversion conditions of Lima, which create an environment that lets particles thrive in the air. This means that cold air is trapped underneath a layer of hot air above, which, combined with the mountain range of the Andes to the east of the city, prevents air contaminants from moving away.

What Is in Lima's Air?

Air pollution is measured by assessing common pollutants that include particulate matter (PM), ozone (O), nitrogen dioxide (NO2), and sulfur dioxide (SO2). PMs are generally particles of dust that come from construction sites, waste burning or wildfires, or industrial-process waste that, due to their diameter, can be easily inhaled. Ozone is a gas produced when a pollutant reacts to sunlight. Nitrogen dioxide is primarily a result of fuel burning, generally produced by the transportation sector, while sulfur dioxide is emitted by fossil-fuel combustion coming mostly from power plants and industrial processes. For these four, the World Health Organization has established air-quality guidelines that provide annual and daily maximum concentrations before they become a threat to health. These guidelines become the standards for many communities to track emissions and execute policies to control or reduce such quantities.

In 2019, Lima published an evaluation of its air quality[47] by analyzing the presence of those pollutants in the air and by relating them to climate conditions throughout the year. The results were obtained with sensors distributed around different city districts and throughout the entire year.[10]

PM10

For particle matter (10) – diameters that are 10 micrometers or smaller – from 2014 to 2017, the city had a yearly average of 50 μg/m3. This is above the 20 μg/m3 annual mean recommended by the World Health Organization.

μg/m3 is micrograms (one-millionth of a gram) per cubic air.

O3

In terms of ozone, the WHO has established a 100 μg/m3 8-hour mean as the maximum suggested and Lima never went over 21 μg/m3 during the daily concentration in all of the sensor stations. However, this is a consequence of the high concentration of NO (nitrogen monoxide) in the air, which quickly destroys the ozone. The study, in fact, showed a slight increase of O3 in all the sensors on a Sunday, suggesting that the reduction of traffic in Lima, which produces NO, reduces the fighting factor to reduce O3.

NO2

In terms of nitrogen dioxide, the maximum recommended by the WHO is 40 µg/m3 annually and a 200 µg/m3 1-hour mean, and this is probably the most evident contaminant concentration in the air of Lima, showing concerning numbers in all of its sensors with a few exceptional months where the concentration was under the recommended 40 µg/m3.

The Ate Station was above 40 µg/m3 in all the measured months, reaching concentrations of up to 191.9 µg/m3 during the month of April. The San Borja Station was above 40 µg/m3, except for the months of September, October, and December (November was not measured). Campo de Marte's station showed numbers higher than 40 µg/m3 in all its measured months, excluding October, November, December, March, and April, which were not measured. Santa Anita Station measured January, February, and May all above 40 µg/m3 with only October at 30.5 µg/m3. The rest of the months were not measured. Finally, Villa Maria del Triunfo's Station showed most of the months above 40 µg/m3, except from June through October.

These high concentrations all throughout the city confirm that these types of contaminants are the main consequence of fuel burning, generally produced by the cars and trucks that move throughout Lima.

SO2

In terms of sulfur dioxide, Lima presented positive measurements below the 20 µg/m3 24-hour mean recommended by the WHO in some of the sensor stations. However, the Ate Station was, in the month of January, at a daily maximum concentration of 45.2 µg/m3 and 22.2 µg/m3 in September; Campo de Marte in May at 22.2 µg/m3, 21.2 µg/m3 in June, and 20.7 µg/m3 in December; Santa Anita at 51.7 µg/m3 in September, 39.6 µg/m3 in November, and 40.6 µg/m3 in December; while Villa Maria del Triunfo was above 20 µg/m3 from May to December. San Borja never went above 14 µg/m3, and Campo de Marte was always under 20 µg/m3 except for the months mentioned above.

The standards set by the World Health Organization are meant to provide guidelines for communities to enforce policies with the goal of protecting public health concerns. These principles are based on rigorous scientific research that provides evidence of the relationship of these pollutants and their effect on peoples' health. However, lowering pollutant concentrations according to their recommendations does not guarantee that the relationship between contaminant and health issues ceases to exist, encouraging communities to adopt measures that lower their concentrations below those recommended numbers by the WHO.

SO_2, for example, has a negative effect on cardiovascular disease and bronchitis; NO_2 causes pneumonia and bronchitis; O_3 worsens asthma problems, reducing pulmonary functions, and may cause permanent damage and even death; and $PM10$ also has an effect on respiratory and cardiovascular disease and on pregnant women: it may reduce the size of the fetus and, once the baby is born, result in a reduction of pulmonary functions, and it is associated with increased mortality rates in all age groups.

Environmental Justice

"Environmental justice" refers to the unequal impact of environmental repercussions, such as floods, contaminated water, or air pollution, in different social and racial groups. This means that populations with the least access to clean water or air quality or where their homes are located in areas that are most vulnerable to natural disasters are usually those with an economic and social disadvantage, compared to the rest of their community.

According to a 2012 Lima Como Vamos Study, the three districts with the highest extreme poverty index were Los Olivos (1.9 percent), Comas (1.4 percent), and San Juan de Lurigancho (0.8 percent),[27] with the last two being part of the most contaminated districts in Lima.[1]

COVID-19

In March 2020, Peru, like most governments in Latin America[23], reacted quickly and declared a state of emergency that produced several measures to control the rates of infection. Lima's air cleared up. The city could be seen from an airplane for the first time in many years, in contrast to when it was covered by a hazy layer of smog that clouded its streets. The restrictions of quarantine to combat the pandemic with social distancing measures impeded people from walking outside or attending gatherings, schools, offices, stores, or restaurants. Borders were closed and remote work and schooling became the norm while teleconferencing made commuting unnecessary.

Lima corroborated that air quality can be rapidly improved if vehicular traffic is drastically reduced and if it reexamines how the industrial sector operates. The city experienced a reduction in the concentration of sulfur dioxide (SO2) from 66 percent during the first week of April to 20 percent during the last week of May in 2020, compared to the same weeks the year before.[49] Nitrogen dioxide (NO2) concentrations also experienced a drop from 40 to below 20 percent, and PM2.5 had a reduction trend during the lockdown of the pandemic.[16]

Nevertheless, this proved catastrophic for the economy, and Peru's economy contracted by around 12 percent, higher than Argentina at 11 percent, and higher than Mexico, Colombia, and Chile, all below 10 percent.[15] In fact, Peru was one of the hardest-hit countries in the region with unemployment and lack of or reduced income. According to the survey "The Early Labor Market Impacts of COVID-19 in Developing Countries," in the Latin American region, 59 percent of respondents reported stopping work in Peru, compared to 50 percent in Colombia, 39 percent in Mexico, and 30 percent in Chile.[23] The hospitality sector suffered, with several businesses closing and losing thousands of jobs. Children without access to the internet or the proper equipment lost track of their classes.

This meant that the lockdown did not necessarily translate into an increased quality of life. For many in the city, especially the most vulnerable sector of the population, the quarantine left them without access to food, education, health services, or general support systems, including the ability to pay for housing. Although this is true for most countries in the world, and especially the Latin American region, Peru and Ecuador were the most affected by the pandemic in economic terms.[43]

The Importance of Improving These Issues

In 2015, 3.6 million people died from burning fossil fuels in the world, out of which more than 190,000 were in the US and almost 40,000 in Latin America.[26] It is a small number, considering the United States' population alone is almost the combined total of Brazil, Argentina, Colombia, and Chile. However, these numbers can and should be lowered.

Cities, in particular, are the areas more vulnerable to air quality issues because they tend to reunite several elements that have a direct effect on the air composition. Factors such as population density, industry, transportation, energy consumption, climatic conditions, large built environments, seasons, and meteorologic conditions such as rain or humidity in some instances amplify otherwise natural air conditions. At the same time, air quality has an impact on the population, which can become a public health issue, affecting productivity and the economy.[17] Air quality can also compromise natural resources by affecting the vegetation structures and behaviors and animal migration patterns, and contaminating food sources.

One factor to consider in air pollution is the amount of time people are exposed to the poor air quality. Contaminated air can cause acute effects if people are exposed for short periods of time or chronic effects when the exposure is long term. In the case of Lima, its geographic conditions worsen poor air quality because of its proximity to the Andes, wind conditions, and lack of rain that confine the air, avoiding the elimination of the polluting particles year-round.

Contamination also exacerbates environmental justice where some sectors of the population in the city experiencing greater impacts from polluting sources therefore suffer greater consequences on their health. According to the 2011 Saturation Study in Metropolitan Lima and Callao, the geographic tendency in concentration of contaminants is toward the North and East zones of Lima due to their proximity to the mountain range to the east and the reduced ability for air to circulate. These areas are also home to some of the more economically depressed communities in the city.

By 2019, the tendency shifted toward the east and south, predominantly in $PM10^{47}$, where the lack of paved roads was a factor contributing to air pollution, showing a connection between higher pollution and communities with limited resources. If Lima persists in improving its air quality, it can induce a positive impact in its economy and generate social benefits.

Lima's Initiatives

Lima's government is aware of the challenges and the responsibilities that come with the goal of providing Limeños with higher living standards, as proposed in its 2020–2024 Institutional Strategic Plan by the mayor's office. Thanks to measures such as the upgrade of the Maximum Allowable Emissions Limits for Motor Vehicle Exhaust to European Emission Standards 2 and 3 in 2001, the beginning of construction of the rapid bus transit (Metropolitano) in 2006, and the implementation in 2011 of the electric train, by 2014, pollution in the air of Lima had been reduced by 50 percent.[29]

And by 2019, the quality of the air had improved by 63.8 percent thanks to the upgrade of the Maximum Allowable Emissions Limits for

Motor Vehicle Exhaust to European Emission Standards 4 in 2017, the implementation of natural gas for vehicles, liquefied petroleum gas, the upgrade of the vehicular fleet, the improvement in the quality of fuels, and the increased use of public transportation.[34] At the same time, Lima has also launched a digital platform to publish real-time data on air quality, which is the beginning step to establish reduction goals.[30]

In conversation, George Castelar Ulfe, Head of the Air Quality and Environmental Assessments Division as part of the Metropolitan Municipality of Lima, understood that recognizing the problem was the first step to overcoming it. "What we do not understand cannot be measured, and what cannot be measured cannot be improved" (Castelar, G., personal communication, April 5, 2022). In 2020, Lima began to implement a low-cost, green, pear-shaped air-quality sensor that recorded data at a fraction of the cost of the original $300,000 reference station (see Figure 4.3). The reduced cost of these new small sensors allowed Lima to spread more of them around the city to assess more, accurate, and real-time data about the air quality. This led to several initiatives, including notifications to citizens about poor-quality hot-spots, best times for different activities, and the visual education about air quality of the community. Lima also focused its efforts on the health of the early-childhood population by deploying sensors in children-attended facilities, such as hospitals, parks, and schools. Castelar's Division also began implementing the first "Área de Emisiones Reducidas" (AER in Spanish) in Peru, which prompted the pedestrianization of 25 percent of Lima's historic center, resulting in a reduction of 40 percent of emissions. However, Castelar noted that they also focused on areas with lower economic resources because "some of the areas with the highest challenges in air quality are those

Figure 4.3 Air Quality Sensors by Municipalidad de Lima

with deficient infrastructure, such as unpaved roads, which increase particles in the air, mostly located in underprivileged neighborhoods" (Castelar, G., personal communication, April 5, 2022).

However, the most drastic improvement came in 2020, during the COVID-19 pandemic that saw PM 2.5 levels of 4 µg/m3 in the San Juan de Lurigancho district on March 20 due to circulation restrictions during the quarantine, which shows that, during the entire month of March, there was no weekly average above 20 µg/m3, revealing that, despite Lima's geographic and climatic conditions, the primary pollutant contributor is the transportation sector.[31]

Evidently, having people quarantined at home permanently is impractical, and in fact proved detrimental to economic development in Peru and around the world, but it does illustrate the possibilities of improving the quality of the air in Lima in the future. The Lima-Callao 2021–2025 Plan of Action for Air Quality Improvement is a plan that has the vision of a Lima that preserves the quality of the city's air by balancing clean sources of energy for the sake of economic development to improve the quality of life of its citizens.

The plan aims to establish strategies that contribute to the decontamination process and promote coordinated efforts for a cleaner city. The plan began with the analysis of the 2020 study on the air quality of Lima to understand the problems in the city in relationship to air quality to establish parameters and goals for the future in the next five years. It also established new air quality standards that determine the parameters, evaluation criteria, and maximum levels for contaminants in Lima's air. It also collected the data of existing meteorologic conditions throughout the city to understand micro-climate characteristics that include air temperature, solar radiation, relative humidity, and wind speed and direction to understand their effect on the air and its composition. The plan measured population density, transportation demand, type of fuels, and types and sectors of emissions.

Understanding all of its existing conditions help conceive its main eight goals, which include to:

- Reduce the contaminants in the air based on their source;
- Reinforce and coordinate the control systems for air quality;
- Provide economic measures to promote clean energy;
- Strengthen the human resources responsible for the management of air quality measures in the city and other governmental agencies;
- Develop and implement informational systems for the community's awareness and participation;

- Prioritize and modernize the public transport systems;
- Encourage research and education about the causes and consequences of pollution; and
- Implement a check and balances system to evaluate the progress of these goals.

In addition, the city has implemented

- A pilot program for traffic congestion with smart traffic lights and traffic volume sensors[53];
- CO_2-consuming billboards[54];
- Upgrades of the vehicular fleet[51];
- A Clean Air Committee[51]; and
- An update of new air quality standards[52].

The government has enacted policies, such as the National Standards for Environmental Quality of 2001 to control pollution through long-term and sustained exposure and the National Alert for Air Contaminant Levels Regulation of 2003 to control acute pollution trough short-term exposure. Both policies reinforce the authority of the Secretary of Health to declare alerts when the concentration of air contaminants exceed or are expected to go beyond the international standards set by the World Health Organization or the National Standards for Environmental Quality.

Ciudad Bicentenario Lima is a new area north of Lima that is looking to become a sustainable model for city development and planning in the region. This project was born out of the Supreme Decree 009–2020 from the Secretary of Environment. This decree stipulated several strategies, including making the Ancón Industrial Park the main industrial node in the country, a transportation hub that will connect Callao with the future Chancay Port, a residential area to house approximately 115,000 people and 2,000 hectares of afforestation area for waste water treatment. This is a unique initiative in Latin America of such a size with a focus on sustainability and resiliency.

The city also introduced the 2040 Lima Metropolitan Development Plan, which addresses air quality in its guidelines. The Development Plan includes tools such as land use regulation, urban mobility systems, open spaces, and urban infrastructure. It also addresses social inclusion, community participation, and the protection of natural and cultural resources. However, the most important principle is the

Table 4.2 by Camilo Espitia, From Information by the International Monetary Fund[16]

Credit Financing and Aid to Small and Medium Size Enterprises	
Country	GDP Percentage
PERU	11.4
BRAZIL	6.2
COLOMBIA	5.7
ARGENTINA	2
CHILE	1.8
MEXICO	1.2

understanding that development is a right that comes with obligations to the common good.

An important factor in the country as a whole is its impetus to increase the investment in the children and the adolescents of Peru. According to the Economic Commission for Latin America and the Caribbean (ECLAC), public spending on the youth increased in Peru from 2.8 percent of GDP in 2010 to 4.2 percent of GDP in 2020, with education being the sector with the largest spending.[16] In fact, in terms of public spending and the protection of small and medium-size enterprises most prevalent in the local communities, Peru was the country in the region with the highest percentage of GDP for credit financing at 11.4 percent – higher than Argentina, Brazil, Chile, Colombia and Mexico (see Table 4.2).[2]

There are Still Some Challenges

The challenges in trying to implement these initiatives are many. There are technological and institutional challenges such as funding, agency accountability, and communication, along with the complexity of allowing a smooth systems-integration at such a scale. Questions will arise: Will investment increase living conditions? Will financing methods incur in property values tax increase? Will it affect housing affordability? There could be apprehension about what could be seen as "the war on the car," with initiatives such as taxing emissions, congestion tolls, reduction or elimination of parking requirements, or charging for parking, and the reduction of investment in road infrastructure for cars, especially if the alternative is not convenient or cost-effective. It is an option for the city to engage the current informal transportation sector in the new mass transit investment opportunities to shift from outdated transit, but it might prove difficult. However, upgrading infrastructure may incur long-term service interruptions that can affect the population.

What Else Can Lima Do?

As a result of the interconnected nature of transportation challenges, traffic congestion, and air quality, several of these initiatives can have a positive impact on other dimensions. The following are suggestions from my research to add value to the efforts that Lima is carrying out to improve its air quality.

Traffic Congestion

Encouraging the use of alternative transportation modes is critical to reducing the dependency on cars. To do this, the city must engage in the following:

- Promoting walkability and incrementing pedestrianized areas;
- Stimulating complete neighborhoods with mixed-use development and increased density;
- Improving and expanding its bicycle lane network;
- Upgrading the coverage, reliability, safety, affordability, and accessibility of mass transit systems such as BRT, rail, or light rail;
- Supporting shared-ride systems;
- Limiting or eliminating parking requirements from new developments;
- Implementing data-gathering devices to adjust decongestion measures in real time;
- Reporting of road incidents for faster response through GPS systems and sensors;
- Including smart traffic lights to streamline traffic and decongest the roads;
- Introducing traffic congestion tolls; and
- Reducing and controlling traffic congestion will inherently have positive results on the air quality of Lima.

Walkability

According to the latest *Lima Cómo Vamos* (How Are We Doing Lima) survey – a program that monitors the progress in several fields in the city's development – only 6.1 percent of the people in Lima think that it is safe to be a pedestrian in the city.[28] An overwhelmingly low percentage.

Complete Neighborhoods

Mixed-use developments mean more services closer to each other, reducing the need for transportation and making walking the primary mode of mobility.

Expanded Bicycle Network

Safe and exclusive bicycle lanes with connectivity to other lanes, services, and other modes of transportation are essential to a reliable use of the bike.

Mass Transit

The current Metropolitano (BRT) covers 26 kilometers[14] and the current Rail Line 1 covers 31 kilometers.[24] In addition, the transport structure needs to extend its services and provide a full integration of the various mass transit systems, including station connectivity, integral service fees, and single-payment methods.

Shared-Ride Systems

Shared-ride systems avoid the wasteful use of a single passenger in a vehicle. Incentives include reduced tolls and dedicated travel-lanes.

Reduced Parking Requirements

Reducing or eliminating parking requirements from new developments have three potential collateral benefits: discouragement of private car ownership; reduction of construction costs that would otherwise go to building garages (potentially lowering housing prices); and leveraging a better use of space, such as public services or community centers. However, eliminating parking requirements must come hand in hand with reliable transportation options.

Traffic Control

As of now, 50 percent of the traffic lights in Lima will be monitored, programmed, and synchronized in real time, thanks to the recent addition of smart lights at 291 intersections in 20 districts of Lima. These smart traffic-lights have sensors that detect the number of vehicles in transit at specific times. These lights will be added to the already 420 intersections out of 1,368 in the city.[33] Previously, one of the challenges to interconnect and create a smart network of lights was that, throughout the process of procurement, different vendors were contracted that carried different models and technologies. A standardization of specifications and contracting city equipment is necessary to ensure a cohesive system.

Air Quality

With public health concerns due to pollution in Lima, reducing GHG emissions is key to improving the city's air quality. As mentioned before, besides traffic control, some of the ways to reduce CO_2 include:

- Sensors to help identify areas of concern in real time;
- Green-space improvement with more green areas and trees;
- Building code requirements for minimum green areas in new developments;
- Urban agriculture strategies;
- Improved waste management;
- Move to renewable energy sources to power the city; and
- Major infrastructure improvement:

   - Airport expansion and additional runways (which have a heavy carbon footprint explained later in this chapter);
   - Callao Port clean power sources;
   - Update its public service vehicle fleets (public transport, emergency response vehicles, and public force) to clean fuel sources; and
   - Taxing on emissions on sectors that pollute to deter further discharge or to encourage cleaner sources.

Green-Space Improvement

According to a 2004 study by the Lincoln Institute of Land Policy, vacant land in Lima represented around 10 percent (6,895 hectares) of its total surface.[11]

This is a great opportunity to incorporate those areas into the sustainable urban development planning strategies for the city. Part of the vacant land can be transformed into green living-areas for the city that can simultaneously serve as public spaces and natural-resource conservation sectors. This includes building-code amendments that require a certain percentage of green areas per development. Incorporating agricultural strategies in the urban setting will reduce gray areas and decrease the need for the transport of produce.

Infrastructure Improvement

Major infrastructure improvement contributes to reducing pollution. The Jorge Chavez Airport Extension plan is a reality. Indeed, it is a much-needed expansion, as the current airport only holds a single runway that increases aircraft congestion in a hub that moved 20,604.250 passengers in 2017.[21] Why is this important for air quality control? According to a 2010 report from NASA, about 25 percent of airplane emissions come from landing and takeoff. That includes taxiing, which is the largest source of emissions in the landing-takeoff cycle.[22] In addition to this, aircraft often have to fly around the city waiting for a permit to land, which also contributes to gas emissions. The contracted expansion, budgeted at $1.5B, includes the design and construction of a second runway and an additional passenger terminal, which will begin operations in 2024.[21]

The Callao Port is the main port in Peru, but its high traffic and operations affect the city's air quality. The operations run while at port, such as boat ballasting and de-ballasting (weight compensation and stabilization by pumping water) and self-unloader boats, could use clean-source power from the port rather than having the boats using their power while docked. Shipping companies would offset the fee of connecting to the port's energy source by saving on the fuels used while docked, guaranteeing the use of clean energy.

Stakeholders Coordination

First, a solid institutional framework is critical as the foundation to execute these policies in the city. Second, the city should conceive a strong set of goals to fulfill the citizens' right to better livability. The public sector, citizenry, private sector, and academia all should move toward a clear goal to achieve the full potential of their tasks of influence and interests.

Connecting Goals with a Timeline

The actual time of plan execution varies substantially, as it includes policy planning and approval, bidding processes, funding planning and sourcing, and in some instances, construction tasks. Nevertheless, establishing goals committed to a timeline contributes to implementation strategies that create a sense of urgency and accountability. The following diagrammatic charts were developed to establish ideas of priorities, time frames, and level of investment per initiative to facilitate a high-level understanding of assessment of stakeholders, scope, and funding for more detailed plans. It is important to commit to critical timelines that may go beyond typical office terms of mayors or other government officials. Policies should be detached from political parties and ideologies to drive projects of such magnitude without interruption.

Lima's Future

Air quality can become one of Lima's emblems of social equity and environmental justice as a city that found the balance between progress and its natural resources. Achieving Lima's economic growth ought not to overrun its natural habitat and there need to be changes in the habits of its citizens that must be supported by policy changes that facilitate those changes. Lima's environmental policies are the key to it becoming a just, inclusive, and healthy city because air quality affects not only our health, but our productivity, food, and water sources. However, this is not only the government's responsibility.

This is everyone's job. Limeños have to play their part to improve the quality of Lima's air, for their own sake, but more importantly, for their future generations. Medellín is an example of citizenry participation by enabling tools that facilitate the conversation between the government and the public and allow their role in the development of the city to be more tangible and have a direct effect on the improvement of their own quality of life. Through technology, an electronic voting mechanism for project prioritization became a pioneering example of public participation in Colombia and the region[5], as we will see in the Medellín chapter.

The future of Lima is in its own hands and its perseverance is its best tool. There is a lot of work to do but there is a substantial track record of the work already done. These accomplishments provide a glimpse of the possibilities of the city's future and that is what should drive the impetus for future planning.

References

1 Andina. (2021) *Infórmate sobre cuáles son los distritos más contaminados de Lima.* Agencia Peruana de Noticias: Andina.
2 Barría, C. (2021) *Coronavirus en América Latina: cuánto y en qué han gastado sus recursos los gobiernos durante la pandemia.* www.bbc.com/mundo/noticias-56949590. Accessed January 24, 2022.
3 Berrone, P. and Ricart, J. (2018) *IESE Cities in Motion Index,* 5(84).

4 Briceño, A. (2018) *El laberinto de los taxis limeños*. El Comercio. https://elcomercio.pe/lima/transporte/informalidad-calles-laberinto-taxis-limenos-noticia-501826-noticia/
5 Cabezas, A. (2019) *Gobierno Electronico y Participación Ciudadana: Análisis de la gestión de la Alcaldía de Medellín en el Plan de Desarrollo Local y Presupuesto Participativo en 2017 bajo el marco del Gobierno Electrónico*. Universidad Federal de la Integración Latinoamericana – UNILA. Foz do Iguaçu: Brazil.
6 Campuzano, O. (2018) *¿Cuál es el Principal Problema Ambiental de Lima?*. El Comercio. https://elcomercio.pe/lima/sucesos/principal-problema-ambiental-lima-noticia-510130. Accessed December 20, 2018.
7 Cardenas, G. (2018) *La ciudad y la basura*. rpp noticias. https://rpp.pe/lima/actualidad/la-ciudad-y-la-basura-lima-retrocede-en-la-lucha-por-controlar-sus-residuos-solidos-noticia-1114285
8 Castillo, G. (2013) *Indicadores Ambientales de Espacio Publico en Bogota*. Universidad Politécnica de Catalunya: Barcelona.
9 City of Buenos Aires Data. (2018) *Superficie de espacios verdes por habitante por comuna. Ciudad de Buenos Aires. Años 2006/2018*. Secretary of the Environment and Public Space: Monserrat.
10 Comision Multisectorial para la Gestion de la Iniciativa del Aire Limpio para Lima y Callao. (2019) *Diagnostico de la Gestion de la Calidad Ambiental del Aire de Lima y Callao*. Secretary of Environment.
11 De Araujo Larangeira, A. (2004) *Tierra Vacante en la Ciudades de America Latina*. (1st ed.). Lincoln Institute of Land Policy: Cambridge.
12 Dextre, J. C & Aranda, F. (2021) *Avanzando con resiliencia: Una nueva movilidad para Lima y Callao*. Pontificia Universidad Católica del Peru: Lima.
13 Diario, C. (2018) *Más de 15 mil limeños al año mueren por contaminación*. https://diariocorreo.pe/edicion/lima/mas-de-15-mil-limenos-al-ano-mueren-por-contaminacion-821584/. Accessed November 28, 2018.
14 Diario La Republica. 2015. Luis Castañeda anuncia nuevo Metropolitano en toda la Vía Evitamiento. [ONLINE] Available at: https://larepublica.pe/sociedad/845530-luis-castaneda-anuncia-nuevo-metropolitano-en-toda-la-via-evitamiento. Accessed December 10, 2018.
15 ECLAC. (2020/2022) *Economic Commission for Latin America and the Caribbean, Preliminary Overview of the Economies of Latin America and the Caribbean, 2021* (LC/PUB.2022/1-P). Economic Commission for Latin America and the Caribbean: Santiago.
16 Economic Commission for Latin America and the Caribbean (ECLAC). (2022) *Social Panorama of Latin America, 2021* (LC/PUB.2021/17-P), Santiago.
17 Gouldson, A., F. McAnulla, P. Sakai, A. Sudmant, S. Castro, C. Ramos. (2015) *La economía de ciudades resilientes y de bajas emisiones de carbono: Lima-Callao, Perú*. Carlos E. Ludeña, (editor), Banco Interamericano de Desarrollo, No. 213: Washington DC.
18 IESE Business School – University of Navarra. (2018) *Cities in Motion*. www.iese.edu/faculty-research/cities-in-motion/. Accessed December 7, 2018.
19 INEI. (2018) *Peru: Estructura Empresarial*. Instituto Nacional de Estadística e Informática. Lima, Peru.
20 INEI. (2018) *Lima alberga 9 millones 320 mil habitantes al 2018*. www.inei.gob.pe/prensa/noticias/lima-alberga-9-millones-320-mil-habitantes-al-2018-10521/. Accessed December 23, 2018.
21 Jorge Chavez International Airport. (2018) *Lima Airport Partners presenta diseño del nuevo terminal aéreo para el Jorge Chávez*.www.lima-airport.com/esp/paginas/noticias-detalle.aspx?idelemento=114. Accessed December 13, 2018.

22. Jung, Y. (2010) *Fuel Consumption and Emissions from Airport Taxi Operations.* (1st ed.). Green Aviation Summit: NASA Ames Research Center.
23. Khamis, M., Prinz, D., Newhouse, D., Palacios-Lopez, A., Pape, U., and Weber, M. (2021) *The Early Labor Market Impacts of COVID-19 In Developing Countries: Evidnce From High-Frequency Phone Surveys.* International Bank for Reconstruction and Development/The World Bank: Washington, DC.
24. Kohon, J. (2015) *Metro de Lima. El caso de la Línea 1.* (1st ed.). Corporación Andina de Fomento: Caracas.
25. Lamas Noriega, R. (2015) *Contaminación del aire en Lima Metropolitana Perú.* www.gestiopolis.com/contaminacion-del-aire-lima-metropolitana-peru/. Accessed December 8, 2018.
26. Lelieveld, J., Klingmüller, K., Pozzer, A., Burnett, R. T., Haines, A. and Ramanathan, V. (2019) Effects of fossil fuel and total anthropogenic emission removal on public health and climate. *Proceedings of the National Academy of Sciences*, 116(15), 7192–7197.
27. Lima Mayor's Office. (2012) *¿Cómo Vamos en Pobreza y Equidad?* Lima Mayor's Office. Lima, Peru.
28. Malpartida J. (2018) *Lima Cómo Vamos: solo el 6% considera que Lima es segura para los peatones.* https://elcomercio.pe/lima/seguridad/lima-6-considera-lima-segura-peatones-noticia-578601?fbclid=IwAR02m-9pcP-4iIkZlIPEVZo21qO2pVyV_IPlC3KGMmqFSlZqpQZ-9FNflrk. Accessed October 12, 2018.
29. MINAM. (2014) *Estrategia para mejorar la calidad del aire ya muestra resultados importantes.* www.minam.gob.pe/notas-de-prensa/estrategia-mejorar-la-calidad-del-aire-ya-muestra-resultados-importantes/. Accessed November 28, 2018.
30. MINAM. (2019) *Calidad de aire en Lima mejoró en más del 60 % en los últimos doce años.* www.gob.pe/institucion/minam/noticias/26607-calidad-de-aire-en-lima-mejoro-en-mas-del-60-en-los-ultimos-doce-anos. Accessed November 28, 2018.
31. MINAM. (2020) *Calidad de aire en Lima durante cuarentena alcanzó niveles que recomienda Organización Mundial de Salud.* www.gob.pe/institucion/minam/noticias/110755-calidad-de-aire-en-lima-durante-cuarentena-alcanzo-niveles-que-recomienda-organizacion-mundial-de-salud. Accessed October 28, 2020.
32. Ministerio Público – Fiscalía de la Nación. (2018) *Observatorio de Criminalidad.* www.mpfn.gob.pe/ observatorio/. Accessed November 11, 2018.
33. Municipalidad de Lima. (2018) *Municipalidad de Lima Instalara Mas Semáforos Inteligente en 20 Distritos.* www.munlima.gob.pe/noticias/item/37202-municipalidad-de-lima-instalara-mas-semaforos-inteligentes-en-20-distritos. Accessed December 8, 2018.
34. Municipalidad de Lima. (2022) *Gestion Municipal de la Calidad del Aire.* Subgerencia de Gestion Ambiental: Lima.
35. Nicolacci, P. (2012) *Movilidad Sostenible: La Bicicleta y su Infrastructura en Lima Metropolitana y Callao.* Pontificia Universidad Católica del Perú. Lima. Peru.
36. Núñez, J. M. (2021) *Análisis espacial de las áreas verdes urbanas de la Ciudad de México.* Centro Transdisciplinar Universitario para la Sustentabilidad (Centrus), Universidad Iberoamericana: Mexico.
37. Orihuela, C., and Rivera, F. (2013) *El costo económico de la contaminación del aire por PM10 en Lima Metropolitana: un análisis exploratorio.* UNALM: Lima.

38 Pinto, V., Gili, R., and Velasco, F. (2015) *Historia del Saneamiento de Madrid.* Universidad Autónoma de Madrid: Madrid.
39 Plastrik, P. and Cleveland, J. (2018) *Life After Carbon: The Next Global Transformation of Cities* (3rd ed.). Island Press: Washington, DC.
40 Redaccion. (2013) Más de 31 mil combis y micros saturan las pistas de Lima. *Peru.* https://peru21.pe/lima/31-mil-combis-micros-saturan-pistas-lima-121691-noticia/#:~:text=Seg%C3%BAn%20la%20comuna%20lime%C3%B1a%2C%20existen,mucho%20para%20lograr%20dicha%20meta. 21 27 August.
41 Redaccion (2014) Sistema de transporte urbano en el Perú genera pérdidas por US$ 20,000 millones al año. *Gestion Magazine.* https://gestion.pe/economia/mercados/sistema-transporte-urbano-peru-genera-perdidas-us-20-000-millones-ano-70604-noticia/. 5 September 2014.
42 Rios, R. and Taddia, A. (2017) *Ciclo-inclusion en America Latina y el Caribe. Guia para impulsar el uso de la bicicleta.* Inter-American Development Bank: Washignton, DC.
43 Schaal, A. and Ardvin, J. (2020) *Covid-19 en América Latina y el Caribe: Panorama de las respuestas de los gobiernos a la crisis.* Organisation de Coopération et de Développement Économiques: Paris.
44 SINIA. (2018) *Superficie de área verde urbana por habitante en Lima Metropolitana.* Secretary of the Environment: Lima.
45 Streimikiene, D. (2015) *Environmental Indicators for the Assessment of Quality of Life.* Mykolas Romeris University, Faculty of Economics and Finance Management: Lithuania.
46 The World Bank. (2020) *Propuesta y recomendaciones para la formulación de una estrategia para la Bicicleta en Lima Metropolitana.* Banco Mundial: Washington, DC.
47 Verastegui, M. V. P. (2021) *Plan de Action para el Mejoramiento de la Calidad del Aire de Lima-Callao 2021–2025.* Secretary of Environment: Lima.
48 WHO (update 2016) *Global Urban Ambient Air Pollution Database.* https://www.ccacoalition.org/en/resources/who-global-urban-ambient-air-pollution-database-update-2016.
49 WHO (2020), *Effects of the Quarantines and Activity Restrictions Related to the Coronavirus Disease (COVID-19) on air Quality in Latin America's Cities.* Economic Commission for Latin America and the Caribbean (ECLAC): New York.
50 World Air Quality. (2018) *Air Quality Index.* https://aqicn.org/map/lima/es/. Accessed October 28, 2018.
51 www.elcomercio.pe. (2017) *El aire de Lima está más limpio pero aún es dañino.* https://elcomercio.pe/lima/sucesos/aire-lima-limpio-danino-425913. Accessed November 10, 2018.
52 www.emgrisa.es. (2017) *Aprobación de los nuevos ECA para aire en el Perú.* www.emgrisa.es/publicaciones/ nuevos-eca-para-aire-en-el-peru/. Accessed November 12, 2018.
53 www.smart-cities.pe. (2018) *La UNI desarrolla semáforos inteligentes para Lima.* https://smart-cities.pe/semaforos- inteligentes-en-lima/. Accessed November 16, 2018.
54 www.youngmarketing.co. (2017) *Vallas Inteligentes Una Apuesta Publicitaria Sostenible.* http:// www.youngmarketing.co/vallas-inteligentes-una-apuesta-publicitaria-sostenible/. Accessed November 14, 2018.

5 Santiago
Energy Efficiency and Sustainability

Tuesday, September 11, 1973. Santiago, Chile
At 11:52 a.m., the house of then Chile's president Salvador Allende, El Palacio de la Moneda, was covered in smoke while two Hawker Hunter bomber planes circled the sky and dropped bombs on the building with implacable force and precision. On the ground, tanks, snipers, and soldiers surrounding the presidential building opened fire, bringing flames out of its windows and putting an end to democracy in Chile. When General Javier Palacios, the senior officer in charge of the undertaking of the house entered the building, his report confirmed the determination to remove Allende out of his post: "Mission accomplished. Moneda taken. Dead President." These words marked the beginning of 17 years of a military regime that, even today, is part of the collective memory of the country. After that, Chile began a series of neoliberal economic policies in response to those completely opposite from Allende's time.

The coup d'état had its origins in the complicated economic context of the country, affected by inflation and currency devaluation, which was a consequence of a global economic crisis that began in the United States. This economic slowdown ended with the 1973 oil crisis which severely increased oil prices to the point of shifting energy consumption from gas to coal due to the elevated gasoline costs.[33] The history of energy use in Santiago has been a critical issue in the agenda of several administrations that have taken innovative initiatives to address sources, consumption, and lately, its residues, including carbon sequestration policies.

But how has the energy sector evolved in Santiago? The switch from gas to electric lighting in the Plaza de Armas in 1883 launched Santiago into the future. Thanks to the use of alternating current, electricity transformed the city and the entire country. The lighting of these first streetlights in the plaza surrounded by the Santiago

DOI: 10.4324/9781003380818-5

Metropolitan Cathedral, the National Historic Museum, the Central Post Office building, and the Santiago Municipality building became a symbol of progress. Soon after, electricity made its way to replace the horse-pulled tramways, and in September 1900, the first electric tramway was inaugurated. In the early 1900s, electricity began to displace gas as the major source for public and private lighting and new development sprung up with the help of electric power in Santiago. By the 1920s, power coverage had grown in the city with the installation of new generators, and in 1921, Compañía Chilena de Electricidad Limitada was born, today known as "Chilectra." Water heaters, irons, and lamps entered the Chilean market to replace coal-based appliances.

Electricity, difficult to explain at the beginning of the century, was often advertised as a "fluid" that represented the overarching concept of progress in technology that also provided the residents with improved public health conditions (less risky than gas and odorless), industrial advancement, and economic prosperity. Electricity was promoted as energy-efficient, durable, and cost-effective. Furthermore, the introduction and spread of electricity in Santiago was activated mostly by the private sector with the public sector serving a smaller part. This in hand propelled the idealization of electricity as a desired commodity that was a symbol of social status and progress, where the costs of electricity could only be absorbed by the more affluent communities in the city.[34] Slowly, the inception of electricity in Santiago and the cultural factors that shaped its implementation as an initial private-driven spread of the network contributed to uneven distribution of resources.

In 1978, the government created the Energy National Commission to develop plans and policies for the development of the energy sector. Four years later, in 1982, the General Lay of Electrical Services was drafted to privatize electricity-provider companies while the state served only as a regulator and controller.

Today, the residential electric consumption in Santiago is 203 kWh/month per household, according to the Energia Region website, where consumption is higher in wealthier communities that have more access to home appliances. Forty percent of electricity in Chile is generated by coal, a percentage that increases when rain does not provide enough for hydroelectric plants, representing a challenge for the country's footprint on the environment.

According to the 2016 study *Estrategia Energética Local Santiago* (Local Energy Strategy in Santiago), between the years 2011 and 2015, 75 percent of the energy consumption in Santiago was based on electricity. In 2020, during the pandemic, electricity consumption increased an average of 44 percent due to more people staying home during the quarantine and the lower temperatures during the restrictions that required the heating of homes.

Since Santiago de Chile is home to 6 million people, representing around 33 percent of the total population in the country, energy efficiency is critical to reducing the city's carbon footprint in the entire country. The first step toward energy efficiency is the ability to reduce energy consumption and the second, to reduce the impact of what is consumed.

In this chapter, we will look at an overview of development in the city and how it has defined energy consumption in Santiago. I will explain the effects of the excess of energy consumption and inefficiency; I will elaborate on the importance of improving these figures and what Santiago is doing to address them.

Santiago's Development

Prior to the arrival of the Spanish colonizers, Santiago was an administrative center of the Inca Empire that used the Mapocho River as its main source for agricultural practices.[3] The Inca settlement was taken over on February 12, 1541, by Spaniard Pedro de Valdivia after a long journey accompanied by 150 Spanish soldiers and thousands of natives from Peru who started mobilizing more than a year before, in January 1540, from the city of Cuzco. The new settlement was laid out under the *Leyes de Indias* (Laws of the Indies) planning principles issued by the Spanish crown just like the ones used for the layout in the Viceroyalty of Lima. Thus, The Plaza de Armas, not far from the Mapocho River, became the center of the settlement. During the mid-1550s, the first large buildings started to appear, and between 1560 and 1580, the settlement's surface tripled,[18] showing the first signs of a city. By the 1700s, the connection between the north and south of the Mapocho River was established, encouraging the expansion of the city.

After its independence in 1810, the city went through rapid growth to establish itself as an important economic center in Latin America, and by the late 1800s, Santiago housed most of the factories in the country, displacing Valparaiso as the economic center of Chile.[2] By the beginning of the twentieth century, to celebrate the first 100 years of independence, Santiago received substantial investment in its infrastructure, including transportation, sewage and water systems, open space, and institutional buildings and services. This investment attracted a workforce from the countryside into the city, which, with the increase in railroad and transportation infrastructure, exploded the numbers of residents in the city. Santiago's center became Chile's administrative hub.

After the Pacific War that ended in 1884, Chile's economy grew, thanks to the additional land annexed from Peru and Bolivia, in a period of growth that lasted until the Great Depression in 1929. This growth period contributed to the investment in infrastructure around the country that allowed for the construction of ports, rail lines, and schools and investment both in the countryside and in its cities. After the 1929 global economic crisis, Santiago's population increased even more from people moving out of rural areas into the city – a common trend in other Latin American capital cities – and its industrial sector slowly recuperated to make up for the world's slow market and lack of resources and replaced it with local manufacturing.[31]

By 1960, the city accommodated close to 2 million inhabitants. By then, rural areas at the periphery of Santiago saw their land absorbed by urban development, and with the hosting of the 1962 World Cup, the city saw even more investment in its infrastructure and economic growth. However, the economy was not moving at the same rate as it did in the first decades of the twentieth century. By the 1950s, the agricultural sector was weak, dominated by latifundium practices that exacerbated inequality in the country, pushing people even further into the city. A series of land reforms began in 1962 to redistribute state-owned land, empowering farmers and dignifying their living and working conditions. These reforms ended in 1973 with the arrival of the Augusto Pinochet dictatorship that reversed them, returning land to private owners and changing the agricultural landscape of Chile.

In 1968, Metro de Santiago was created to then become one of the largest in Latin America, transforming the urban landscape of the city. In 1979, a new Urban Development National Policy (PNDU) opened up real estate development to respond to market pressures, causing an increase in land prices, an expansion in the city's urban footprint, a shift of more people to the periphery of the city, a housing crisis, and segregation (Sabatini, 2000). The expansion encouraged the taking of previously agricultural land on the periphery of the city to be used for housing developments, which rapidly increased the number of residents and energy consumption in the city. The expansion of the city's footprint increased the necessity of infrastructure expenses – mainly vehicular infrastructure, such as the Circunvalación Américo Vespucio – that the government had to incur, leaving the building of the city in charge of the private sector.

Similar to Mexico City, Lima, Bogotá, and several other Latin American cities, the unregulated development of Santiago and the housing quality disparities that came out of the Urban Development National Policy triggered the No. 31 Supreme Decree of 1985, known as "Adjusted Policy," which attempted to correct the consequences of the privatization of development. Some of the premises of this new decree included acknowledging the limited available land, introducing planning for the city's growth to avoid the threats of social and environmental resources stemming from unregulated development driven by market forces, and the public participation in such planning process. However, the inequalities created during these decades persisted, and by the year 2000, the spatial disparities in the city's composition were evident, with the highest-income groups living in smaller numbers of the 34 communes of the city, while the most vulnerable socioeconomic groups were being spread out across the territory.[21]

In 2010, the government created the Secretary of Energy by separating it from the Secretary of Mining in order to elaborate and coordinate policies in Chile's energy sector, which contributed to energy efficiency improvements. For instance, that same year, through a public-private nonprofit partnership, the ACHEE agency (Chilean Agency of Energy Efficiency) was created to help reduce the intensity of energy consumption in Chile, maintain sustainability, become a global reference of energy efficiency, and transform the topic into a cultural value of the country.

The agency (later renamed Sustainable Energy Agency in 2018) has contributed to the improvement in energy consumption and efficiency in public buildings of Santiago, including the Secretary of Justice and the National Institute of Statistic.[23]

Energy Consumption in Santiago

As of 2006, energy consumption in the Metropolitan Region was distributed in the following sectors: mining, 2.4 percent; commercial, 7.3 percent; residential, 23.4 percent; industrial, 26.3 percent; and transportation, 40.5 percent.[19]

Ten years later, in 2016, the mayor's office in Santiago and the Secretary of Energy produced a study called Santiago Local Energetic Strategy in order to design policies that contribute to energy efficiency, the use of alternatives energy sources, and emissions reduction. The study revealed that, out of the 2.016.726 MWh of total energy consumption in Santiago, 1.521.060 MWh is mainly based on electricity whose primary consumers are the commercial and industrial sectors, followed by residential consumption that comes from several plants largely powered by coal.[7] The study, however, omitted the transportation sector in its measurements because its scale and area of operations expand outside the city boundaries in a regional range and prevented the study from having a fixed reference point to determine accurate consumption and greenhouse emissions.[26]

According to the 2008 Consumption Characterization and Estimate of the Potential Energy Savings in Different Regions of Chile by the University of Chile, the commercial sector is composed of companies dedicated to electricity, water, gas, construction, commerce, restaurants, hotels, communications, finances, services, banking, and public administration, while the industrial sector is composed by cement, food and beverage, textile, steel, paper, fishing, and mining, among other industries.

In terms of residential consumption, the city's 2016 study also revealed that energy consumption in the residential sector goes up during the winter season for dwelling heating; however, most of the households use petroleum-based fuels, which supports the theory that electricity consumption has risen due to the increase of household appliances. The residential sector shows apartment units increasing its consumption, which coincides with the number of building permits in the same period of time in the city between 2011 and 2015.[30] In addition, single-occupancy dwelling units have been on the rise, increasing the ratio of home appliances per person and square footage. Where a family of four would have a single refrigerator or microwave, single-occupancy units mean each occupant has the same number of appliances. Nevertheless, on average, heating systems represent 29 percent and water heaters, 30 percent of the amount of energy consumed in the residential sector. These numbers increase during winter.

The Santiago Commune is the fourth most populated commune in the Santiago Metropolitan region but the one with the highest electrical residential consumption in the nation.[24] The sales of apartment units has been greater than those of houses by almost three times on a yearly average since 2016, especially of units between 50m2 and 70m2.[11] The demand of smaller residential units, including smaller single family housing units, indicates an overall increase in energy consumption per household in the city.

With an area of 22.4 km^2 and a population of 404,495, the number of households in the commune amounts to 193,628, composed of 77.3 percent apartments, 16.7 percent houses, and 5.7 percent single-room dwelling units, mostly representing overcrowded conditions for the less-privileged or immigrants.[25] Santiago emits a total of 689,719 T CO2 eq. Of GHG, mostly coming from the electricity source (see Table 5.1), while almost 80 percent of the energy consumption comes from electricity (see Table 5.2).

Both, Tables 5.1 and 5.2 indicate that the production of electricity should come from clean sources to reduce the impact on the environment.

Where Do Santiago's Energy Sources Come From?

Sixty percent of the power in Chile is generated by thermoelectric plants, followed by almost 30 percent hydraulic plants, with smaller contributions from wind and sun power at 10 percent, and an even smaller 0.08 percent for geothermal-generated power.[7] According to the Secretary of Energy, Santiago's Metropolitan Region received electricity from hydroelectric, diesel petroleum, biomass, and solar sources. However, the region is currently focusing large investment

Table 5.1 Santiago Commune Emissions by Camilo Espitia (Based on Estrategia Energética Local Santiago 2016)

Santiago Commune Ghg Emissions in T CO2 eq.

Energy Source	Industry	Residential	Municipal	Total
Electricity	370,106	139,106	17,075	526,287
Natural Gas	26,722	13,474	746	40,942
LPG	*22,435	*22,435	*22,434	67,304
Kerosene	0	140	0	140
Solid Waste	*18,349	*18,349	*18,348	55,046
Total	**437,612**	**193,502**	**58,603**	**689,719**

* Amount was given as a whole source emission. An assumption of equal emissions per sector was taken to assess an approximate quantity specifically for the residential sector.

Table 5.2 Santiago Commune Consumption by Camilo Espitia (Based on Estrategia Energética Local Santiago 2016)

Santiago Commune Energy Consumption

Energy Source	Mwh/Yr	% of Consumption
Electricity	409,339	79.7
Natural Gas	70,409	13.7
LPG	26,204	5.1
Kerosene	7,425	1.5
Total	**513,377**	**100**

in solar energy, which includes the Til Til, Melipilla, and San José de Maipo projects. As of 2015, the 52 communes of the Santiago Metropolitan Region were powered with 871 MW generated by mostly Nueva Renca Thermoelectric with 379 MW at 43.5 percent, Central Alfalfal Hydroelectric with 178 MW at 20.4 percent, and smaller thermoelectric plants that represent 6 percent. However, since the commune's electricity transmission and distribution of power depends on substations, a shift from power distributer to power generator with clean sources could supply the commune with clean air, lower prices for consumers, and funds that could stay in the commune.

Thermoelectric plants, also known as coal-powered plants, use coal to heat water that produces steam to power turbines. These turbines are then connected to a generator that spins to generate electricity. This energy source presents two challenges. (Since water is used as part of the process, even in closed loop systems, some water is lost in the evaporation process.) The dependency of water presents this power generation method with the vulnerability of water scarcity that will have an effect on the power generating capacity of thermoelectric plants. At the same time, coal burning is detrimental to air quality.

However, because of its affordability due to its vast availability and cost-effective transportation and storage, it remains the most popular energy generator in the world, producing around 37 percent of global electricity, according to the World Coal Association. Coal combustion emits sulfur dioxide (SO_2) and nitrogen oxides (NOx), forming small particles that increase respiratory and cardiovascular diseases that increment the risk of mortality.[12]

In contrast, non-conventional, renewable energy sources self-generate and regenerate from the natural processes of the earth, including solar, wind, wave power, small hydraulic plants, biofuels, and geothermal energy. Biomass sources include the use of wood, agricultural waste such as corn or sugar cane, biogenic material such as municipal waste, and animal and human waste. These are converted into energy through combustion (burning) to produce heat, thermochemical conversion to solid, gaseous, and liquid fuels, or biological conversion to liquid and gaseous fuels. The use of biofuels helps reduce the carbon emissions from fossil fuels.

Importance of Energy Consumption Efficiency

Because of the implications of energy production, energy efficiency and the extent of consumption are critical to reduce economic, social, and environmental risks. Chile imports 98 percent of its primary consumption of crude oil, 75 percent of its primary consumption of natural gas, and 96 percent of the consumed coal.⁴ Chile's energy dependency on foreign sources of power is a burden on the country's economic resiliency. At the same time, the topic of energy security, given its main sources, is inherently tied to environmental resiliency and the country's capacity to evolve and adapt to issues such as climate change, global warming, or pollution, where the encouragement of clean energy sources provides the country with a local power supply that is also beneficial to reducing the carbon footprint in an increasingly consuming society.[22] Simultaneously, because fossil fuel sources are diminishing, looking for renewable sources is critical for the future of any community.[6]

According to a Universidad de Chile 2008 report on Chile's energy consumption, the largest consumer is the transportation sector at 40.5 percent, followed by the industrial sector at 26.3 percent, the residential sector at 23.4 percent, the commercial sector at 7.3 percent, and the mining sector at 2.4 percent. At the same time, 74.7 percent of the city's GDP comes from the commercial sector and 16.9 percent from the industrial sector.[19]

There is, not surprisingly, a positive correlation between the level of productivity and the amount of energy consumption.[17] This means that the expansion of an economy's GDP is strongly linked to higher energy-consumption levels. The more productivity, the more energy is consumed. This is important to balance the control and reduction of energy consumption without compromising economic prosperity in the city. In essence, energy efficiency is critical for both sustainable economic growth and resilient environmental development.

In Santiago in particular, according to Obrecht (2016), there are vast differences in energy affordability and coverage in the most vulnerable sectors of the city.[15]

Effects of Uncontrolled Energy Consumption

The first step to mitigating the negative effects of energy consumption is to reduce consumption itself. It requires behavioral changes at individual, private, and public levels. Regardless of the efficiency of an energy source, reducing it is the most important step toward sustainability and resiliency. Uncontrolled energy consumption is a threat to sustainable development. Even though the energy consumption in China and India is elevated, their consumption per capita is lower than the world's average of 2.4 kW/person in 2007.[17] However, the consumption per capita in Chile has been higher that the world's average since the year 2000.

When it comes to social justice, the reduction of residential energy consumption and the use of renewable energy sources for energy can represent lower costs and a wider access to services for lower-income residents, reducing the impact of inequality in Santiago – not to count the environmental advantages of energy efficiency. For example, electricity consumption in the public sector in the metropolitan region in 2006 represented 44.75 percent of the total electricity consumption in the city, while oil-based energy sources represented 44.75 percent.[19] Lowering excess consumption can contribute to municipal budgeting for other critical needs for Santiaguinos.

The world's average electricity consumption per household in 2010 was 3.5 MWh/year (or 291 kWh/month), according to World Energy Council.[32] However, it is challenging to understand what the minimum consumption should be as different countries vary their coverage, source, household size, and daily habits. In Santiago, the monthly residential electricity per household is 206 kWh/month,[14] in Lima is 190 kWh/month,[16] and in Mexico City is 88 kWh/month.[29] Even with these statistics per city, it is also difficult to use another community as a measuring standard, since there are different alternatives to provide for daily habits. There are communities that still rely on wood fire for cooking and heating; there is gas as an alternative for water heaters and cooking; and in some instances, although in small numbers, some households are not connected to electric meters[1], which may skew actual electricity or total energy consumption.

However, energy burden is typically greater for low-income households who tend to spend more of their income on energy.[10] Access to energy sources that are safe and affordable means vulnerable populations will have the same opportunities of quality of life. However, without reducing consumption and efficiency, energy procurement has negative effects on all community members.

Santiago's Initiatives

Since the transportation sector is the largest energy consumer in the city, addressing mobility as an urban-planning tool is the most critical step to reduce consumption and become energy efficient. In 2013, Santiago created the 2025 Santiago Transportation Master Plan that includes a vision of urban development that reduces the inequality in the distribution of investment among the 52 communes of the Metropolitan Area. Part of the goals, similar to the Lima's 2025 Transportation Master Plan, include the reduction of traffic congestion and the inclusion of an electric fleet of trains and buses to reduce the impact on the environment (see Figure 5.1).

Figure 5.1 Electric Bus by Cristian Silva Villalobos
Source: Shutterstock.

The Santiago Plan also includes urban development strategies that increase the density of the city and mixed-use development, especially around transportation nodes. The investment in transportation, according to the Plan, would be in areas with already high population numbers or in areas where there were projections for a large amount of housing development, which constitutes an advancement in the usage of public transportation, which reduces energy consumption. The Plan also set as objectives the ideas of promoting and supporting the use of alternative modes of mobility, like bicycles and walking. The Plan also discusses remote working, flexible working schedules, shared rides, and smart city technologies, all focused on reducing energy consumption and pollution.

In 2014, Chile began taxing energy companies that keep using non-renewable sources for power generation for their emissions unless they move into clean sources or include CCS (carbon capture and storage) technologies in their current infrastructure. The idea behind the tax is to encourage energy companies to shift their efforts towards clean energy sources. This is done by measuring the emissions to assess the amounts to be taxed.[20]

In 2016, the Lastarria neighborhood started the "Ruta Lastarria – Bellas Artes Carbono Neutral" project, which formed a cultural and gastronomic corridor that compensates its CO2 emissions to become the first carbon-neutral neighborhood in Chile (see Figure 5.2). The corridor looks at strategies to reduce greenhouse gases coming from fuel consumption, electricity use, and waste. The participating restaurants and cultural facilities in this corridor reduce carbon emissions by compensating them using carbon bonds or green bonds, which were financial incentives provided by the Chilean Utility Company Colbun. The neighborhood is already a pedestrian-only corridor, which in itself is an energy efficiency for mobility in the area, reducing emissions and improving the quality of life of residents and visitors.

As of 2017, Chile already had 17 percent of its energy produced by nonconventional, renewable sources, increasing from 7 percent in 2014 with the goal to increase it to 60 percent by 2035, out of which 76 percent represent solar-power projects in currently in progress.[5] In Rethinking Infrastructure in Latin America and the Caribbean by Fay et al., in the first decade of the 2000s, the country had 34 research centers developing research on energy, out of which 15 were in the metropolitan region, where the main research area was nonconventional

Figure 5.2 Lastarria-Bellas Artes Corridor by Diego Grandi
Source: Shutterstock.

renewable energy.[4] Around 55 percent of the country's research and innovation budget is executed in the region where the innovation-manufacturing industry has developed clean technologies and the implementation of energy resources and recycling. At the same time, as part of the Clean and Sustainable Region goals, the city encourages the use of clean energy sources as a strategic regional objective as part of the 2012–2021 Regional Development Strategy.[9] Since 2014, Chile has gone from 5 percent to 19 percent of nonconventional renewable sources in the electric-generation sector.[27]

Santiago Tembici Itau Bikes is a shared bicycle system that has 2,500 bicycles and 190 stations around Santiago, which include solar energy to power the docks (see Figure 5.3). The system includes an application to see different convenient route-options to improve the efficiency of the trips and encourage the use of active mobility in the city. It lays out trips on bicycle lanes, available bikes and docks at the stations, and estimated travel time. By encouraging active mobility, the city reduces energy consumption in the transportation sector.

The Energy Sustainability Agency (ESA) and the Secretary of Energy created the *Educa Sostenible* (Educate Sustainable), an educational program that includes community engagement in teaching proper energy use. In 2022, in the Metropolitan Region of Santiago, the program distributed printed material with Energy Sustainability, guides, games, and resources for all levels education.[28] This contributes to shape the future generations about energy use, efficiency, and policy.

As of 2018, the ESA has also provided energy-supply kits to communities in Santiago located in energy-isolated areas. The kit includes a photovoltaic panel, battery pack, LED lanterns, and a solar-rechargeable radio. At a national level, the programs of the ESA have encouraged renewable energy-production and energy efficiency that have reduced consumption of 14,000 MWh/year and reduced greenhouse gases by 5,600 tons of CO_2, as well as the granted 32 Energy Efficiency Seals to several organizations that contributed to the savings of 591,505 MWh/year, equivalent to the energy consumption of 77,462 homes per year.[23]

The city also engaged in upgrading municipal buildings to make them more energy efficient by increasing insulation values in building facades, upgrading windows, adding shading devices in patios to reduce heat, and adding solar panels. Not only does this improve the energy consumption in the buildings, but in educational institutions, students improve their performance due to a healthier and comfortable environment.

Figure 5.3 Santiago e-Bikes Itau by Fotos593
Source: Shutterstock.

Perhaps one of the most ambitious initiatives from the Chilean government that shows its commitment to addressing energy efficiency is the issuance of a sustainability-linked bond in the London Stock Exchange, tied to the commitment to reduce carbon emissions and increase investment in renewable-energy sources with more than half of electricity coming from a clean source.[13]

Santiago in the Future

The city already has plans for a 30 percent reduction in its greenhouse gas (GHG) emissions by the year 2030 in the industrial, commercial, and municipal sectors for the decrease in CO2 emissions.[25]

In 2014, the government created the Energia 2050 initiative as a way to design and execute a long-range energy policy with social, political, and technical support for the energy efficiency of the country. Some of the goals from this document include 100 percent of vulnerable households in Chile having continuous and high-quality access to energy by 2035. Also, by 2035, the initiative aims at 100 percent of new homes and 25 percent of existing ones complying with thermal comfort and lighting new standards. The initiative also strives for improving public participation in the conversations of energy efficiency and the reduction of costs of energy access to vulnerable households. By 2050, all of the country's planning and zoning development tools should be aligned with energy policies so new development improves its efficiency by following building and zoning codes.

The country also hopes to have at least 70 percent of its national electricity generation coming from renewable sources. Chile's expectations include to become an energy-efficiency services exporter, to unbind energy consumption from economic growth, and to have the commercial sector, responsible for 95 percent of energy consumption, report and manage their greenhouse gases following the standards set by the country to measure emissions – all by 2050 (among other goals).

As of 2020, most of the projects in construction for energy generation were photovoltaic sources, and several approved projects in the SEIA (Environmental Impact Evaluation System), including *Parque Fotovoltaico Bollenar, Nueva Central Solar Fotovoltaica Mandinga, Planta Fotovoltaica Nahuén, Nueva Central Solar Fotovoltaica* San Ramiro, *Nueva Central Solar Fotovoltaica* MACAO, and *Parque Fotovoltaico Rucasol.*

In addition, there are several solar-roof projects spread out throughout Santiago, including the San Borja, San Juan, Padre Hurtado, and Barros Luco hospitals with a total capacity of 430 kW, as well as the

Museo de la Memoria (70 kW), *Palacio de la Moneda* (30 kW), *Liceo Industrial Eliodoro García Zegers* (30 kW), and *Teleton Santiago* (70 kW).[14]

The Latin American Region in general is doing well in terms of supplying energy by means of clean sources. In fact, according to the World Bank, the region's electricity component is the cleanest in the world. Although, most of the electricity is generated by hydroelectric plants in the region, investment to support wind power increased in Brazil, Chile, Mexico, and Peru, and to a lesser extent in Colombia, Ecuador, and Uruguay.[8]

The challenge is that most of them are coming from hydroelectric plants vulnerable to climate change, which causes droughts and risks the provision of energy. At the same time, Chile has room for improvement because the region scores well in investment in general, thanks to higher percentages of investments in smaller countries, such as Nicaragua and Panama, while Chile falls behind these countries, including Peru, although it outperforms Mexico, Argentina, Colombia, and Brazil.[8]

Additional investment could come from the 2014 energy emissions tax fines, collected from noncompliant companies, which could be routed toward new, clean technologies for power generation. Additional funding can be achieved through financial penalties to commercial buildings (including office, retail, and residential buildings) that do not comply with the application of building codes that look to drastically reduce GHG emissions.

Diversifying the sources from which electricity is acquired such as wind, solar, or biomass is critical to providing a resilient and sustainable source of electricity. However, energy efficiency is not only important in reducing the impact on the environment. It is also critical to social justice because it can represent a cost savings for many vulnerable families. Energy efficiency represents social justice for a city with drastic temperature changes, where in the coldest and hottest months, many families do not have access to the same comfort and shelter or suffer the economic pressure of heating and cooling their homes. This also includes access to hot water or the need to use methods that can affect their health. During COVID-19, many families transferred their cooling and heating needs from the workplace and schools to their homes, leading to energy injustice.

Chile has the infrastructure capacity and the political will to lessen energy consumption, decrease GHG emissions, and drastically reduce the impact on the environment. With the participation of the public and private sectors, it is possible to achieve the 80-percent reduction in GHG emissions for Santiago to be an energy efficient and socially just city. What the city does today will shape the future for the upcoming generations. Santiago's reduction of energy use will be essential for a better city today, but most importantly, for a welcoming, kind, and inclusive city tomorrow.

References

1. Cruz, G. and Duran, M. (2015) *El consumo de energía eléctrica en los hogares de México por nivel de ingresos, 2012*. Universidad Autónoma Metropolitana: Mexico City.
2. Canto, J. (1895) *Boletin de la Estadistica Industrial de la Republica de Chile 1894–1895*. Sociedad de Fomento Fabril: Santiago.
3. Castillo, S. (2014) *El río Mapocho y sus riberas: Espacio público e intervención urbana en Santiago de Chile (1885–1918)*. Ediciones Universidad Alberto Hurtado: Santiago de Chile.
4. CONICYT-Union Europea. (2007) *El Sector De Energía En Chile. Capacidades De Investigación Y Areas De Desarrollo Científico-Tecnológico*. Chile: Santiago.
5. Diario la Tercera. (2017) *El 17% de la energía producida en Chile proviene de fuentes renovables no convencionales.* www.revistaei.cl/2017/04/24/17-la-energia-producida-chile-proviene-fuentes-renovables-no-convencionales/#. Accessed July 26, 2019.
6. Dudley, D. (2018) *Renewable Energy Will Be Consistently Cheaper Than Fossil Fuels By 2020, Report Claims*. Forbes Magazine: Jersey City.
7. Emol Staff. (2018) *De Norte a Sur: Revisa dónde y quiénes generan la electricidad que le da energía a Chile* www.emol.com/noticias/Nacional/2018/02/08/894243/Revisa-donde-y-quienes-generan-la-electricidad-que-prende-Chile-de-Norte-a-Sur.html. Accessed December 18, 2018.
8. Fay, M. Andres, L. Fox, C. Narloch, U. Straub, S. and Slawson, M. (2017) *Rethinking Infrastructure in Latin America and the Caribbean: Spending Better to Achieve More*. (1st ed.). World Bank Group: Washington, DC.
9. Gobierno Regional Metropolitano de Santiago. (2012) *Estrategia Regional de Desarrollo 2012–2021*.Gobierno Regional Metropolitano de Santiago: Santiago.
10. Hernández, D. and Bird, S. (2010) Energy burden and the need for integrated low-income housing and energy policy. *Poverty & Public Policy*, 2, 5–25.
11. Hurtado, J., Lozano, F., and Robles, O. (2020) *Informe Inmobiliario Gran Santiago*. Publicación Cámara Chilena de la Construcción A.G.: Santiago.
12. Koplitz, S., Jacob, D., Sulprizio, M., Myllyvirta, L., and Reid, C. (2017) *Burden of Disease from Rising Coal-Fired Power Plant Emissions in Southeast Asia*. ACS Environmental Science and Technology: Washington, DC.
13. London Stock Exchange. (2022) *The London Stock Exchange congratulates The Republic of Chile for the issuance of the world's first sovereign Sustainability-Linked Bond*. London Stock Exchange: London. www.londonstockexchange.com/discover/news-and-insights/london-stock-exchange-congratulates-republic-chile. Accessed August 14, 2022.
14. National Commission of Energy. (2022) *Región Metropolitana de Santiago – Energy Data*. https://energiaregion.cl/region/RM. Accessed October 21, 2022.

Santiago 89

15 Obrecht, R. (2016) *Caracterización del Consumo Energético en la Region Metropolitana y Analysis de Escenarios de Eficiencia Energética*. Universidad de Chile: Santiago.
16 OSINERGIM. (2015) *Informe de Resultados Encuesta Residencial de Uso y Consumo de Energía*. ERCUE 2014–2015: Lima.
17 Pastén, C. (2012) *Chile, Energia y Desarrollo*. Georgia Institute of Technology: Atlanta.
18 Pena Otaegui, C. (1944) *Santiago de Siglo en Siglo: Comentario Histórico e Iconografico de su Formación y Evolución en los Cuatro Siglos de su Existencia*. Primera Parte. Empresa Editora ZigZag: Santiago de Chile.
19 PRIEN. (2008) *Caracterización del Consumo y Estimación del Potencial de Ahora en Energia en las Distintas Regiones de Chile*. Universidad de Chile: Santiago.
20 Reuters Staff. (2014) *Chile becomes the first South American country to tax carbon*. www.reuters.com/article/carbon-chile-tax/chile-becomes-the-first-south-american-country-to-tax-carbon-idUSL6N0RR4V720140927. Accessed October 31, 2018.
21 Rodriguez, A. and Winchester, L. (2001) *Santiago de Chile. Metropolización, globalización, desigualdad*. University of Birmingham: Birmingham.
22 Romero, N. P. (2011) *Consumo de Energía a Nivel Residencial en Chile y Análisis de Eficiencia Energetica en Calefacción*. Universidad de Chile: Santiago.
23 Santelices, I. and Lopez, F. J. (2019) *Agencia de Sostenibilidad Energetica Reporte 2028–2019*. Secretary of Energy.
24 Secretary of Energy of Chile. (2015) *Comuna Energetica – Santiago*. www.minenergia.cl/comunaenergetica/?p=888. Accessed December 18, 2018.
25 Secretary of Energy of Chile. (2015) *Estrategia Energetica Local Santiago*. (1st ed.). Secretary of Energy: Santiago de Chile.
26 Secretary of Energy of Chile. (2016) *Estrategia Energetica Local Santiago: Para la Toma de Decisiones Energéticas en el Territorio*. Municipalidad de Santiago: Santiago.
27 Secretary of Energy of Chile. (2017) *Estudiantes de la Región Metropolitana imaginaron la energía del futuro*. https://energia.gob.cl/noticias/metropolitana-de-santiago/estudiantes-de-la-region-metropolitana-imaginaron-la-energia-del-futuro. Accessed July 26, 2019.
28 Secretary of Energy of Chile. (2022) *Autoridades dialogan con 13 comunidades de Educa Sostenible en Renca y entregan material educativo en energía*. https://energia.gob.cl/noticias/metropolitana-de-santiago/autoridades-dialogan-con-13-comunidades-de-educa-sostenible-en-renca-y-entregan-material-educativo-en-energia. Secretary of Energy: Santiago.
29 Secretary of Energy of Mexico. (2020) *Consumo de electricidad por hogar*. www.biee-conuee.net/datamapper/#electridad-por-hogar.html. Accessed December 14, 2020.
30 Valderrama, R. (2018) *Transformación Urbana en Santiago de Chile: Politicas de Escala y Coaliciones de Poder*. Universidad Autónoma de Barcelona: Barcelona.
31 Valenzuela, B. (1984) *Caracterización Industrial de la Metrópoli de Santiago de Chile*. Pan American Institute of Geography and History: Mexico.
32 Wilson, L. (2014) *Average Household Electricity use Around the World* http://shrinkthatfootprint.com/average-household-electricity-consumption#g48DRWmOB6T3OgrS.99. http://shrinkthatfootprint.com/average-household-electricity-consumption. Shrink That Footprint. Accessed December 19, 2018.

33 Yáñez, C. and Garrido-Lepe, M. (2017) *The Third Cycle of Coal in Chile, from 1973 to 2013: From Climacteric to Rejuvenation.* Universidad de Valparaíso: Chile.
34 Zacarías, Y. (2021) The electric fluid and the search for materiality: Visions of energy and technology in the advertising of the first electric lights. Santiago, Chile. 1900–1920. Diseña, 18, Article 3.

6 Buenos Aires
Food Security and Urban Agriculture

Like a mournful carnival in the middle of November 2001, millions of Argentinians participated in a *cacerolazo*, a pot-and-pan-banging demonstration from inside homes out their windows protesting the announcement of banking restrictions imposed by the International Monetary Fund (IMF). The new regulations came after years of loans and financing to the Argentinian government without precautions about the level of debt the country had accumulated for decades. The restrictions consisted of freezing US-dollar-dominated accounts and assets and limiting withdrawal amounts, due to the devaluation of the Argentinian currency.[33] The demonstrations evolved into marches through the streets of Buenos Aires, demanding peoples' savings be returned, as banks closed their doors and emptied their savings due to the financial restrictions. The roaring metal sounds of the pans turned into protests, and several financial institutions were destroyed, and thousands lost their lifelong savings. This was the result of years of economic stagnation that began in 1998, which resulted in an economic, institutional, political, and social crisis. With the economy lagging, the country decreased the value of its currency, and this devaluation encouraged the production sector to increase prices on products because their exporting value became the reference for local commodities. Argentina, a food-exporting nation (the first soybean flour, second peanut, and third soybean and corn exporter in the world[6]), experienced higher prices on local products and an increased difficulty for low-income families that exacerbated food insecurity in its own territory.

After the economic crisis of the early 2000s, the National Plan for Food Security (PNSA) was created through the Secretary of Social Development to improve nutrition in the country. The crisis also contributed to the potable water and sanitation utilities being returned to the government after having been privatized in 1989. Remanding

DOI: 10.4324/9781003380818-6

operations to the state was due to a general discontent about the private sector not meeting the initial expectations of service and coverage.[23]

Later in 2009, the government launched the Universal Appointment per Child, a monthly stipend per child under 18.[1] The local government also maintained the efforts to improve food security for its residents, and by 2015, around 12,000 families in Buenos Aires had a monthly food subsidy through the Ticket Social program, consisting of a deposit made on a card that is used at participating vendors.[14]

Unfortunately, COVID-19 increased the disparities of food access in Buenos Aires.[24] The impact of the pandemic increased the number of people in need of meals and affected many of the community kitchens' productivity due to mobility restrictions and the reduced stock of food. In Buenos Aires, almost 18 percent of the community kitchens closed their doors, while only 30 percent were able to meet the increased demand.[4] At the end of 2020, Argentina had 63 percent of the infant and adolescent population living in poverty, while its community kitchens collapsed due to the increased number of people trying to access food due to the loss of jobs and school meals.[39] Nevertheless, Argentina's Food Bank increased more than 50 percent the kilograms of food provided between 2019 and 2020 and an increment in the plates of food from 19.4 million in 2019 to 22.6 million in 2020.[4]

Buenos Aires has had challenges in providing itself with the tools to have the concepts of urban development and agricultural production coexist within the same area. However, it has recently begun implementing policies that help promote food production within the city to reduce the inequalities of food access.

Bringing closer the availability of food to the community is the first step toward guaranteeing food accessibility. The farther the food sources, the less cost-effective, less fresh, and less sustainable the food business-model becomes, making the other aspects of food security harder to accomplish. Food security in urban settings must use urban planning as one of the mechanisms by which, through land use, zoning, and transportation, a city can address food access and environmental justice. Ironically, the first human settlements began to function around agriculture; however, over time, agriculture and cities grew apart as separate concepts.

According to the 2018 National Census, Argentina has 37,411,993 hectares of arable land, with the Central-West Region (Cuyo) having more than 95 percent of the cultivated area in the country. This includes the provinces with the highest production: Mendoza and San Juan – far from Buenos Aires, the biggest urban center of the country.

In this chapter, we will look at an overview of the development in the city and how it has defined food security in Buenos Aires. I will explain the effects of the deficient food security in the city; I will elaborate on the importance of improving these numbers and what Buenos Aires is doing to improve this.

Buenos Aires' Development

Originally a city that was part of the Viceroyalty of Peru, Buenos Aires had two foundations. The first one, in 1536, by Spanish conquistador Pedro de Mendoza, who named it *Ciudad de Nuestra Señora Santa María del Buen Ayre*. The second (and permanent) one was on June 11, 1580, by also Spanish conquistador Juan de Garay, who changed the name to *Puerto de Santa María de los Buenos Aires*. Under this name, the city became the capital of the Viceroyalty of Rio de la Plata in 1776, which, due to its geographic location and port condition, became an important political focal point in the relationship between the kingdoms of Spain and Portugal.

Prior to the creation of the viceroyalty and before becoming an important port city in the Americas, Buenos Aires had goods brought from Europe through the Port of Lima, which, due to its great distance and the time required to get such goods, contributed to the increase of merchandising smuggling from the closer Portuguese territories (now Brazil) on the new continent.[2] The status of "capital city" gave new geopolitical power to the Buenos Aires, which encouraged economic development and important infrastructure investment such as roads and channels, as well as the building of significant institutions such as customs, the post office, the Buenos Aires consulate, and the trading market.[2] As a port city, Buenos Aires enjoyed the benefits of being the central point of everything that went out of and came into the country, including food production (see Figure 6.1).

The urban fabric of the city developed at a fast pace, and by the end of the 1800s, Puerto Madero and Dock Sud opened, making Buenos Aires the largest port in Latin America by the early twentieth century. After Argentina's independence in 1816, Buenos Aires extended its boundaries, and by the end of the century, European migration into the city exploded. The new European influx gave the city a more urban character and helped populate the country as whole. The lower numbers of inhabitants in Argentina during colonial times was due to the resources of the continent being located predominantly in Mexico and Peru, which had attracted larger populations.

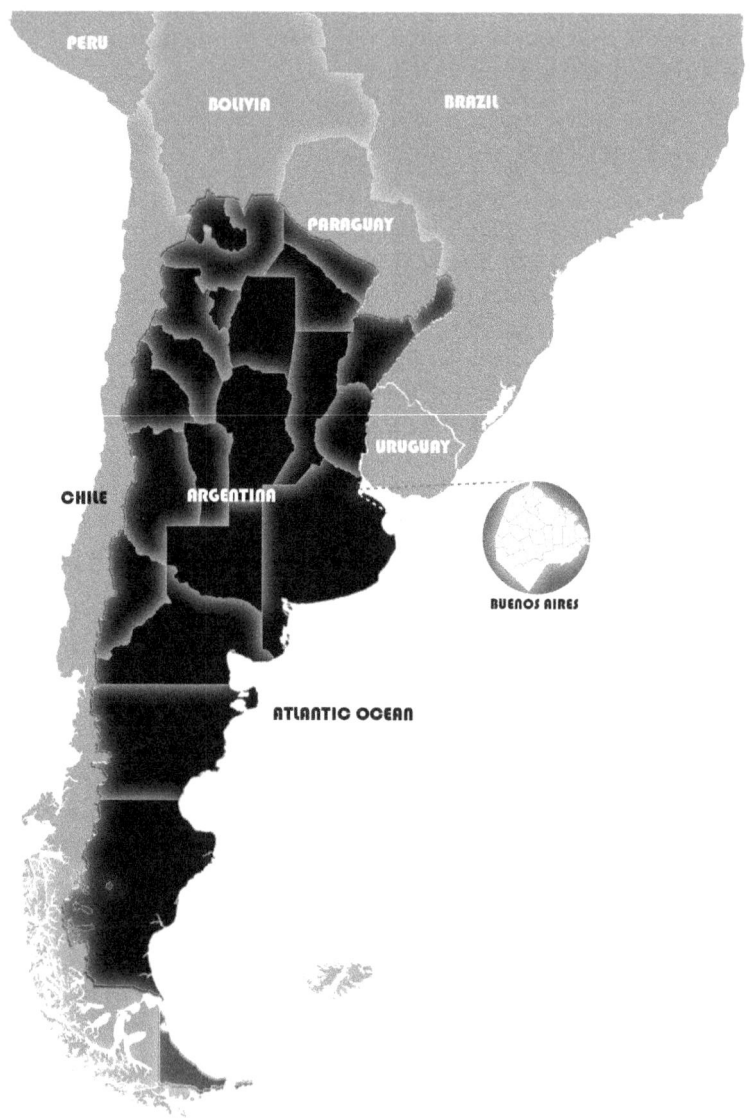

Figure 6.1 Buenos Aires Location as Export City by Camilo Espitia

The port and its economic power began to expand immigration, trade, and pluricultural ideas only comparable to those in European cities. The need to provide housing for the incoming population changed the city's layout and the previously large homes became smaller, narrow, and elongated and known as "*casas chorizo*" that allowed for the flexibility of multiple rooms with independent entrances. This was one of the physical manifestations of the transition from the colonial city to the modern city.

This sudden population growth left the city short of infrastructure and with growing slums, which contributed to thousands of deaths in 1871 due to yellow fever. Buenos Aires' migration patterns increased the amount of people on its streets at a faster rate than Mexico City, Bogotá, Lima, or Santiago. For instance, Mexico City had 225,000 inhabitants in 1870 and 471,066 in 1910; Bogotá, 78,000 in 1898 and 116,951 in 1912; Lima, 100,516 in 1876 and 140,000 for 1908; Santiago, 195,612 in 1875 and 403,775 by 1907; and Buenos Aires, 196,052 in 1870 and 1,300,000 in 1910.[35]

In 1876, the government introduced the *Ley de Inmigración Avellaneda* (Avellaneda Immigration Law) to promote more European immigration and attract a workforce. In 1880, the city became the federal capital of Argentina. A healthy economic relationship between the British Empire and Argentina in the first decades of the twentieth century brought infrastructure investment in the country that resulted in a large railroad network connecting Buenos Aires with the rest of the country, facilitating the exchange of products between the two countries. This caused migration from the rest of the country into the city, which pushed people into the periphery of the city, and by the 1950s, shanty towns started proliferating on the outskirts.

Prior to World War I, Argentina had its transportation infrastructure modernized, especially a strong expansion of its railroad network. In 1880, the total length of rail lines in the country was 1,563 miles, and by 1914, it reached more than 21,000 miles.[37] In 1913, the first Latin American underground transportation system opened as a way to mitigate the increasing traffic in the city, promoting suburban development and even greater growth in Buenos Aires.

After World War II, Argentina's economy grew to supply manufactured and agricultural products to European countries, all of which had Buenos Aires as their transition point. This increased the number of laborers in the city but also brought the *Estatuto del Peón Rural* (Rural Worker Act), which gave rights to rural workers, including minimum salaries and maximum work hours and vacations, given the growing demand for agricultural products in the world. These incentives for rural labor were parallel to the union movements, since the number of urban workers began to grow, especially in Buenos Aires. This period of growth ended in the middle of the 1950s, which brought Argentina an economic crisis after a coup against then-President Juan Domingo Peron in 1955.

It is around this decade where the expansion of the city became more evident with the proliferation of self-built housing at the periphery of the territory with the help of the deficient official controls, while multifamily housing sprang up in larger numbers.[19] These self-built settlements occurred mainly on land that was previously dedicated to agriculture, straining the connection between urban dwellers and food resources.

During the 1970s, the city suffered rent-market deregulation, and the government began investing in public housing, which relocated low-income families from the self-built housing into public-funded housing projects. This caused the dislocation of the relationship between housing and employment that had organically occurred previously. For around two decades, this triggered higher inequalities in the city, and by the 1990s, the *Villas Emergentes* (Emergent Villas) doubled.[19] Globalization and the new economic structures created during the decade of the 1990s, in addition to the economic crisis of the early 2000s, contributed to transforming the urban land-structure of the city.[25] According to the National Institute of Statistics and Census (INDEC), in 2001, 53 percent of people in the Grand Buenos Aires area lived below the poverty line, but by 2010, that number went down to 5.8 percent.[8]

However, even though poverty levels were decreasing, inequality was still an issue afflicting the city. By 2010, out of its 14 million residents,[11] the south of the city had a mortality rate 20 percent higher, a life expectancy four years shorter, and a fertility rate 50 percent higher[36] than the other parts of the city. The same year, Argentina had 1.6 million undernourished people.[10]

Because the center of the city, unlike other cities in Latin America, remained the focal point of development and the socioeconomic heart of Buenos Aires, low-income families moved toward the periphery – mostly toward the south – while the central, wealthy population expanded toward the north, close to the coast of the La Plata River, with healthier landscapes and the capacity to access services, including food.[14] This resulted in an unequal built-environment, with some residents living with a shortage of green, high-quality spaces, and with some areas having difficult access to food.

However, in 2017, the *Plan Estratégico Participativo Buenos Aires 2035* established goals that included the increase in spaces and policies to guarantee support of the practice of healthy nutrition, including measurement practices such as the percentage of families that have been able to incorporate such practices and the reduction of senior citizens' food insecurity by 30 percent.[14]

Current Food Security in Buenos Aires

According to the 1996 World Food Summit, food security exists when all people, at all times, have physical and economic access to sufficient, safe, and nutritious food that meets their dietary needs and food preferences for an active and healthy life. There are four dimensions that help define food security. The first dimension is the physical availability of food, which refers to the actual production capacity of a community and its agricultural proficiency; the second one is the economic and physical access, referring to the relationship between income and prices and the community or individual's ability to access and acquire the available food production; the third one is food usage, referring to the nutrition practices and food-preparation habits of the community or individual once it has accessed the food; and finally, the fourth dimension refers to the stability of food availability, access, and utilization on a continuous and uninterrupted basis.[9]

Food-access inequality in Buenos Aires is manifested in the high cost of food and the country's food-export model, both of which leave local residents with lower-quality and over-processed food, affecting their access to proper nutrition. Argentina's food insecurity is anchored in access and distribution rather than supply and production. This is contrary to other countries, where severe climate events, such as drought or cold waves, affect supply or events, such as in Bolivia, which has been affected by flooding due to El Niño.[30]

Even though 55 percent of agricultural land is dedicated to the production of soy,[43] only 16 percent is consumed in Argentina. The remaining 84 percent is processed and sent out of the country. This has other consequences that include the reduction in the farming of other products more common in the diet of residents, such as corn and wheat.[7]

The country, however, has enforced programs to mitigate its food-access problems. The ProHuerta Program has been operational for 12 years under the responsibility of INTA (National Agricultural/Livestock Technology Center). It is financed by the Secretary of Social Development and assisted 3.2 million people in the country in 2002.

According to the Food and Agriculture Organization (FAO) in 2014, Argentina improved food distribution in the entire country and was among the countries with the best performance in the elimination of poverty and hunger and the reduction by half of the percentage of people suffering from hunger.

Buenos Aires joined the Milan Urban Food Policy Pact in 2015 with more than 100 cities in the world to develop sustainable food systems that guarantee healthy and accessible food, protect biodiversity, and reduce waste. The "*Cuidemos los Alimentos*" (Let's Protect Food) initiative was born out of the commitment to this pact and the United Nations Sustainable Development Goals as a coordinated committee that included the General Secretary and International Relations, Secretary of Citizen Development, Secretary of Environment and Public Space, and the Environmental Protection Agency.

In January 2018, Buenos Aires created the *Programa de Agricultura Urbana* (Urban Agriculture Program) to promote urban agriculture through the city's Environmental Protection Agency as an economically viable production and consumption system – sustainable and with social justice. In specific, the program looks to promote and train green jobs, research and develop sustainable growing methods, compost, encourage the production of healthy food in different parts of the city, encourage community participation, coordinate with different government agencies, generate stakeholder exchanges – including academia – and create a database of local farms and volunteers. In the end, given that the program is an urban agriculture-project means that its greater opportunity is to tackle the challenge of access and distribution of food that the country faces.

One remarkable project stemming from this program is the Paseo Ambiental Sur in Villa Soldati, with four greenhouses that generate fruits and vegetables that provide produce to local communities in the neighborhood. This space serves an educational tool to grow knowledge about environmental issues in the city. It consists of wetlands with local fauna and flora, along with renewable-energy technology to demonstrate the possibilities of coexistence between nature and urban life, including urban agriculture.

In 2019, as part of a social program, the Rodrigo Bueno neighborhood created the Organic Nursery (*Vivera Organica*) to promote the culture and relationship to local land that, later in 2020, produced the first totally organic harvest, allowing it to be economically sustainable (see Figure 6.2). This initiative was spearheaded by the Housing Institute of Buenos Aires and the Secretary of Human Development. This space also provides education and training on local flora and the restoration of natural systems within the urban context.

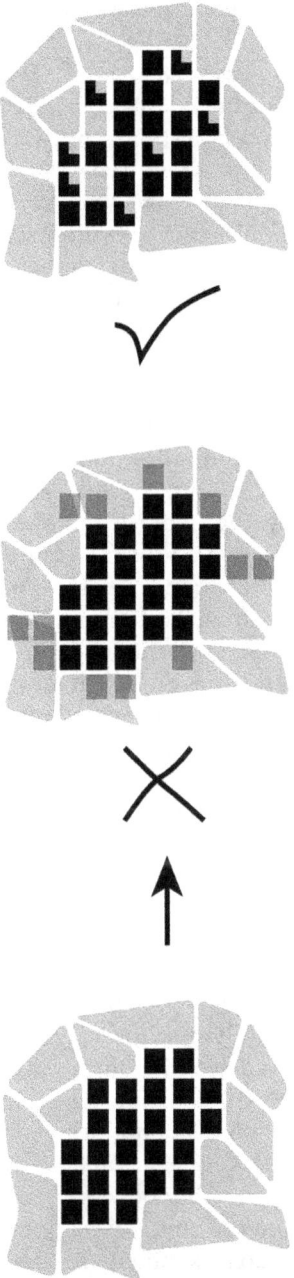

Figure 6.2 Urban Farming Diagram by Camilo Espitia

In concept, the city understood the need of expanding food sources within the city rather than expanding the city toward areas typically used for food production.

A different program, *Argentina Contra el Hambre* (Argentina Against Hunger), which was begun in 2020, provides food security for the most vulnerable population in the country, including mothers starting at three-months pregnant, children up to six years old, and people with disabilities. This initiative involves no paperwork, and children and mothers automatically enter into the system to receive the funds and are removed once the child turns seven. This program includes a "*Tarjeta Alimentar*," a card with funds deposited monthly, school meals, and financial support for community kitchens, public markets, and agriculture.

The *Lanus Libre de Hambre* (Lanus Free of Hunger) movement was founded on February 15, 2020. The initiative started with a Map of Hunger that was then transformed into a Hunger Fighter Map. Before the movement initiative, around 36,000 food rations were served daily in this municipality. By August of the same year, the number of daily rations grew to around 80,000 through support received from the state and additional funds from the Lanus Municipality to also support the older more traditional community kitchens.[12]

In December 2020, the government of Buenos Aires created Law 6377 to promote urban agriculture. This law is intended to become the legal support to transform underused public and private land by granting permits for the use of agriculture within the city's urban fabric. Some of the advantages of this law include the impact-reduction of food production, sustainability practices to reduce the city's carbon footprint, and community participation.

Unfortunately, COVID-19 exposed food access issues for thousands in Buenos Aires, despite the city's efforts to reduce hunger. During the quarantine restrictions, the population that depended on walking out on the streets for income had few options to protect themselves from the virus. The dilemma for many *Bonaerenses* was whether to submit to hunger or the COVID-19 virus.

The challenge of food security during the COVID-19 pandemic, however, is not exclusive to Buenos Aires. In 2021, 22 percent of Medellín's citizens at some point during the pandemic included households where at least one member ate less than three meals because there was not enough food, especially in the lower socioeconomic households (*estratos* 1 and 2).[20]

Nevertheless, Argentina extended the national food emergency until December 31, 2022 as a response to the economic slowdown.[10]

The number of programs that the country, and specifically Buenos Aires, have implemented show that there is a desire to confront food security; however, it might be worth it for the city to take a closer look at all the initiatives and make sure there is no duplicate or disparate effort that may hinder progress.

Food Security in the World and Its Importance

Sadly, the world wastes approximately 1.3 billion tons of food a year, representing 30 percent of the consumed food, according to the Food and Agriculture Organization (FAO) of the United Nations. Ady Beitler, founder of Nilus, a tech company that helps distribute products that the supermarkets typically discard at affordable prices to fight against food insecurity, affirms that, unfortunately, food is wasted because it is too aesthetically unappealing to be stocked in supermarkets, the packaging is broken – even if the food itself is in a good state – or the expiration date is nearing and it does not get purchased. Food is also wasted because it spoils due to inappropriate storage and because of excess or inadequate food preparation. Latin America represents 10 percent of the waste, while residents of Buenos Aires waste 8.4 kg a year, or 2.9 kg per resident, which in 2016, represented 9,500 tons in the city that year.[15] The places where food is wasted are in residences, supermarkets, and restaurant and food establishments, from patrons who prefer not to take leftovers home.

Although there is no comprehensive data on the amount of waste per country or city in the Latin American region, one common trend is the waste between the postharvest and distribution steps due to the lack of infrastructure, which affects transportation, handling, and storage in the process.[3]

Between 2011 and 2013, there were 842 million people with undernourishment problems. The Southern Asia region had 295; Sub-Saharan Africa, 223; Eastern Asia, 167; South-Eastern Asia, 65; Latin America and the Caribbean, 47; Western Asia and Northern Africa, 24; Developed Regions, 16; Caucasus and Central Asia, 6; and Oceania, 1 (see Table 6.1). Within the Latin American region during the same period of time, however, Argentina had less than 5 percent of its population undernourished.[40] In fact, according to the Food and Agriculture Organization, food security in Latin America has improved since the early 1990s, with more than 30 million people overcoming hunger since 1992. However, Peru has been the most successful country in the region, thanks to the Compromiso 5x5x5, a program committed to reducing the slow development of children five years old or younger

Table 6.1 People With Undernourishment Between 2011 and 2013 by Camilo Espitia

People With Undernourishment Between 2011 and 2013

Region	Number (Million)
Southern Asia	294.7
Sub-Saharan Africa	222.7
Eastern Asia	166.6
South-East Asia	64.5
Latin America and the Caribbean	*47.0*
Western Asia and Northern Africa	24.3
Developed Regions	16.0
Caucasus and Central Asia	5.5
Oceania	1.0
Total	**842.3**

Source: Data from the United Nations.[40]

by 5 percent in a period of five years. These policies reduced malnutrition from 28 percent to 13 percent between 2006 and 2016.[29]

Food security is important because of its inherent relationship to health. The CDC (Centers for Disease Control) established that health is determined by genes and biology, health behaviors, social and environmental characteristics, and health services or medical care. Food availability is determined by environmental and social factors, while its consumption habits are a reflection of health behaviors in the individual. Since the social and environmental determinants are the factors that can be more easily controlled to reduce the efforts that have to be made on medical care, it makes sense that food security is treated as a public health issue. Public health is not only about doctors, insurance, medicines, or hospitals. Dr. Geof Rayner and Emeritus Professor of Food Policy at the City University of London Tim Lang, in their work "Ecological Public Health: Reshaping the Conditions for Good Health," argue that public health includes the relationship between people and their environment and propose five models on which public health could be conceived to shift investment and improve the results of public health.[28] In all five models, food security can be found as an element of public health.

Model 1 Sanitary-Environmental

This model is based on the idea that health is affected by external environmental factors. A city's infrastructure is considered an external factor that can have an effect on an individual's health. Hence, the framework for the production quality, transportation affecting its freshness, and manipulation of food would be essential to meet the demands of the proper sanitary and environmental conditions for good health. It is a good example of what Mexico City has been dealing with in terms of its water infrastructure, which Buenos Aires should address as part of its food security issues.

Model 2 Social-Behavioral

Rather than external factors affecting health, this model focuses on social and cognitive areas of the individual. It refers to the individual's behavior and attitude toward the body based on the assumed awareness of the harm or benefits of such behavior. This model sees education, literacy, and lifestyles as factors that affect health. Educating people about healthy habits is essential under this model, which includes knowledge of food preparation and manipulation of products as factors included in food security.

Model 3 Biomedical

This model bases its approach on medical science to understand the unseen factors that affect health as internal and external to the body. Under this model, understanding bodily functions reacting to internal or external factors is key to the improvement of health. Understanding how the body responds to certain types of foods is also important to food security.

Model 4 Techno-Economic

This model focuses on the concept of health being a result of political, economic, and societal development as factors that improve or decrease the quality of health of individuals. It sees economic and knowledge growth as factors that improve livability standards, which improve health at the same time. This model argues for health related to improved quality-of-life that includes access to resources like infrastructure, sanitary reforms, and proper food sources to promote better nutrition.

Model 5 Ecological Public Health

This model examines the relationship of humans with the natural world. Despite the fact that humans have evolved to a state of "control" of the environment, this model still sees the cohabitation and coexistence with the natural environment as essential to understanding humans as part their environment rather than its master. It addresses the fact that human actions have an effect on the environment, and at the same time, any change in the environment will have an effect on humans. It addresses our relationships with other species (plants and other organisms), which may have an effect on our resource availability.

An entire health system refers not only to medical care but also to directly or indirectly related factors such as housing, hygiene, access to medical assistance, food security, and nutrition. Unfortunately, it is a problem where the youngest population is at higher risk because, the younger the infant, the more vulnerable to environmental factors like climate conditions, infections, air quality, or food sources.

There are also economic advantages to food security. Proper access to healthy food can reduce the costs of medical treatments arising from malnutrition and contributes to daily functions, such as learning and working. According to doctors Deanna Hoelscher and Alexandra Evans, lack of access to proper nutrition affects public health, which, at the same time, affects the US economy. In children, poor nutrition affects their education, which can have a negative impact on employment and earnings in the future.[17] Personal and social development may be affected due to poor school performance, which may have a long-term effect on their subsequent academic life. This can eventually translate into disadvantages in the skills that could otherwise contribute during their productive professional life. This impacts social mobility because the level of educational achievement has an effect on future career opportunities, including positions and salaries.[22] The competitive traits of a community or a city as a productivity-center may be compromised as a consequence of food insecurity.

Who Should Be Part of the Conversation?

The role of the government is an important one, but it is not the only interested party that can tackle food security. There are several stakeholders involved in guaranteeing healthy food policies and food security, including the coordination of media as a tool for the divulging of healthier habits and concerns, the private business sector with programs that benefit their employees or the communities they serve or are located in, government agencies with the execution of policies and monitoring, and academia with research, education, and the training of society in bringing the issue to light.

Food security, as mentioned before, is not only about the accessibility of food, but the capacity to consume quality nutrition, which requires comprehensive policymaking to reduce the risks of unhealthy nutritional behaviors. This means that even international economic policies in product trading should encourage the availability of healthy products that are low in fat and sugar and promote fruit and vegetable production to improve on public health-concerns locally. International trade agreements should acknowledge local eating habits and product availability to make sure economic interests do not overshadow those of local health-concerns. At the same time, local policies, such as controls on the advertising of unhealthy products, will prevent issues such as obesity and malnutrition, as well as the health conditions that arise from them.

One of the ways all these stakeholders can contribute together toward food security is through the topic of urban agriculture.

How Does Urban Agriculture Improve Food Security?

There are several tools to address food security, but in this chapter, we will focus on urban agriculture because it is the one tool planners have the ability to manipulate through zoning and land use ordinances that can bring food closer to the people.

The increase in population and economic challenges have created urban settings with higher risks of food insecurity, and thus, urban agriculture becomes an important engine for food production in cities. "Urban agriculture" refers to farming practices in urban settings with reduced areas. It contributes to food security because it increases the offer of healthy food and reduces the number of distributors typically found in the economic model between farm and citizen, which helps reduce prices and the shelf life of products.

Due to the increasing rates of urbanization in Latin America, and specifically Buenos Aires, population growth has reduced the capacity to provide food security for all its inhabitants. The reduced spaces in cities for food production within their urban footprints increases the challenges of food access and the dependence on market conditions for purchasing capacity. With low employment and no local food sources, urban residents are vulnerable to food insecurity.

Given that Argentina's food security challenge is about access and distribution and not production[21], how much land does Buenos Aires need to have in its urban footprint allocated for agriculture to guarantee access to food to low-income residents? Can roofs be the underused real estate that can provide the space for agriculture? How complex is it to operate and maintain community gardens? Should agricultural land at the periphery be protected from the market pressures of development? How much land should the city allocate to match the calorie intake suggested by the WHO for proper nutrition and to guarantee food security for the people of Buenos Aires and to reduce the dependence on land outside the city? Should the concept of vertical farming be part of the equation when discussing urban agriculture?

The World Health Organization suggests that a proper diet should include at least 400 grams, or five portions, of fruits and vegetables per day[42], while 1 square foot can yield 0.5 pound (226 grams) of mixed vegetables and small fruit crops.[27] This means that, to yield 400 grams, you would need 1.77 square feet of land per person.

The 2010 census revealed a population in the metropolitan region of 14,819,137 people, which means it would take 26,229,872 square feet (2.43 km²). This is approximately equivalent to 300 soccer fields for the proper 400 grams of fruit or vegetables for citizens. As of today, the city has 412 soccer fields, not counting professional stadiums.[38] Furthermore, compared to the amount of green space that the city offers, it is possible to provide food for the citizens in Buenos Aires. As of now, there are more than a thousand green areas that have a total area of 19 km² – including 43 parks, 240 plazas, 383 small plazas, 316 road medians, 31 gardens, and 42 spaces with other descriptions.[16]

This hypothetical calculation of minimum land purposed to agricultural that is required to provide a minimal portion of fruit or vegetables for a healthy diet in Buenos Aires is only an argument for the feasibility of providing food for all in the city. But it is also an argument for the relationship between food production and city planning and the importance of urban agriculture as a means of social justice. City planning should consider natural-resources management, including food sources and production, as part of its resiliency. In fact, the city already promotes the Itinerant Neighborhood Supply Fairs (FIAB), which go around green spaces in the city and provide high-quality products at affordable prices. This is step forward to leveraging open space as area to supply food, even if it is for now just on a rotational basis.

There are several successful examples in Latin America of organizations that have implemented urban-agriculture policies and have been able to reduce the risks of food insecurity and other inequity issues in urban centers. The Botanical Garden in Bogotá has started an urban-agriculture project that trains and supports sustainable development, food security, and social and economic development.⁵

In 2021, Bogotá approved the Bogotá Cundinamarca Metropolitan Region Law to implement a regional master plan that integrates the fair trade of food resources from farmers in the region.

In 2020, Caracas began the "Plan Siembra Ortalizas" (Grow Vegetables) in the Organopónico Bolívar 1, an organic garden founded in 2003. The program's objective is to tackle inflation in food prices to guarantee access to fresh products.

Quito began in 2016 the AGRUPAR project (Participative Urban Agriculture) resulting in employment creation, income improvement, and the promotion of sustainable development in the city.³¹

Honduras began a project in neighborhoods on the perimeter of Tegucigalpa that were chosen because of their poverty levels, safety issues, food insecurity, state presence, limited public services, and land availability. Something particular about these projects is that 88 percent of the participants were women who were part of training programs on water and soil management, water collection methods, irrigation, food security and nutrition, soil, and tools and equipment for growing their own food. The result was an increase in vegetable and fruit consumption and health improvement.¹³

Belo Horizonte has implemented aggressive measures to improve food security in the city with policies that include urban agriculture with high success-rates through agroecology and programs in low-income communities to grow food in backyards and community gardens since 1993. Thanks to Municipal Law No. 6352, 1993, the city also implemented food assistance programs and food production by promoting farmers' markets and regulated prices to preserve accessibility while implementing changes in its food-supply system to support and provide food to organizations, local restaurants, and food banks to feed the school population and vulnerable residents in general.²⁶

Challenges in Agriculture

The concept of urban agriculture is not really new to cities. In fact, the first human settlements began tied to agriculture as one of humanity's first efforts to modify its environment. This practice allowed nomadic groups to remain in one place and begin the first established societies that then develop more complex achievements such as trade, language, and writing. Because of the faster growth of cities, agriculture began to be separated from denser communities and food production deemed challenging to supply the growing numbers of people.

Currently, agriculture, especially in urban settings, is facing challenges that compromise the capacity of cities to promote food production within the urban fabric, affecting food accessibility. Food waste is a global problem that misuses about a third of the food that is produced in the world throughout the process that starts from production and ends in consumption, according to the United Nations World Food Program. Since this region has food-waste challenges due to lack of infrastructure, investment is necessary to reduce the time, distance, and logistics of distribution and transportation. Food waste is not only about the food itself that is wasted throughout the harvesting and distribution process but about everything that is involved in such a process, such as water and supplies used in the process. As of 2020, the region was wasting 220 million tons of food a year.[3] Urban food production is necessary to bring food closer to residents and reduce waste and prices for the people of Buenos Aires (see Figure 6.3).

Another challenge that food production faces is climate change and global warming. Temperatures and the amount of sun and rain are some of the factors that have an effect on agriculture. The increasing population numbers of cities mean higher consumption of resources, energy, and production of greenhouse gas emissions that contribute to global warming.[41] In addition, water availability, plant disease, and pests have irrigation and plant-development implications that affect the yield

Figure 6.3 Urban Farming Buenos Aires by Andrés D'Elia

a crop may have.[34] Fortunately, the recent Plan de Acción Climática 2050 Ciudad de Buenos Aires (PAC 2050) has made climate change a priority in its future development, with the main objectives being a carbon neutral, resilient, and inclusive city by 2050. However, one of its action-steps focuses on sustainable nutrition by supporting urban agriculture and fairs to promote a healthier quality of life. The plan also aims at promoting the Urban Agriculture Program and hydroponic crops in the Environmental Information and Education Center, promoting local gardens in low-income neighborhoods, creating the "Healthy Living Strategic Plan" and "My Healthy School Program," implementing gardens and nurseries in public schools, expanding organic and vegan food festivals, and increasing the sales of fruit and vegetable bags.[32]

Reduced spaces and sun exposure in urban settings that allow for food production are also challenges that Buenos Aires and all cities face. Typically, the larger the crop, the greater the productivity the crop yields.[18] However, there are several alternatives for urban agriculture methods that reduce the amount of land required for cropping. Some of these methods include mixed cropping, hydroponics, aeroponics, aquacrops, and aero-hydroponics. A complementary way to reduce the amount of land for cropping is vertical farming, which started in the 1800s in the midst of the industrial revolution.

Some early examples of vertical farming include Machu Picchu, the settlement about 75 kilometers from Cusco, the capital of the Inca Empire, whose terraces allowed it to maximize the land available for farming. Nowadays, vertical-farming technologies include the capacity to manipulate artificial temperature and lighting indoors to enhance the performance of what can be grown. With limited space, vertical agriculture is a tool that cities should leverage to increase food production inside the urban footprint and reduce the dependance on outside communities and the impact on the environment.

Food Security in Buenos Aires Tomorrow

Buenos Aires is creating the space and policies to provide the food that makes the city equitable. Part of the journey is making sure the city sees food as part of its built, social, and economic environment. Food production and urban environments are no longer separate concepts. As part of its economic development goals in the Buenos Aires 2035 Plan, Buenos Aires has an overarching goal of ending hunger and achieving food security for all, improving nutrition, and promoting sustainable agriculture. As part of its urban-resiliency goals, Buenos Aires wants to encourage responsible consumption-habits and behaviors toward the environment and natural resources to increase the production of food within its urban footprint.[14]

For a country with such a capacity for food production and a city with the motivation and policies directed toward bringing food closer to its residents, Buenos Aires has a promising future of food security. Addressing nutrition with constant and affordable access to food can be undertaken by the use of urban planning as a social-justice measure. Zoning codes that require minimum open spaces, encourage urban food-production, and promote physical access to healthy food is part of how the city can increase food security. Residents of Buenos Aires should not have to depend on the charity of organizations to access food and this is the opportunity for city planners to transform the quality of life of millions in the city.

References

1 Abeyá, E. O. (2016) Una evaluación crítica de los programas alimentarios en Argentina. *Salud Colectiva*, 12(4), 589–604. doi: 10.18294/sc.2016.935.
2 Almandoz, A. (2002) *Planning Latin America's Capital Cities 1850–1950*. Routledge: London.
3 Alonso, J. (2020) *América Latina y El Caribe pierden 220 millones de toneladas de alimentos al año*. Deutsche Welle www.dw.com/es/am%C3%A9rica-latina-y-el-caribe-pierden-220-millones-de-toneladas-de-alimentos-al-a%C3%B1o/a-55111025. Accessed August 27, 2021.
4 Banco de Alimentos. (2020) *Reporte 2020*. www.bancodealimentos.org.ar/reporte-2020/. Buenos Aires, Argentina. Accessed August 27, 2021.
5 Bogota Mayor's Office. (2018) *Directorio de Huertas Urbanas de Bogota DC*. Universidad Distrital Francisco José de Caldas: Bogota.
6 Bolsa de Comercio de Rosario. (2020) *Podio mundial de exportaciones: ¿Qué lugar ocupa la Argentina?* https://bcrnews.com.ar/mercados/en-cuales-productos-argentina-esta-en-el-podio-mundial-de-exportaciones#:~:text=Con%20respecto%20al%20podio%20mundial %2C%20soja% 2C%20girasol%20y%20peras. Bolsa de Comercio de Rosario. Accessed August 27, 2021.
7 Calzada, J. and Rossi, G. (2016) *84% de la soja argentina se exporta como grano, harina, aceite y biodiesel*. Bolsa del Comercio de Rosario: Rosario, Argentina.
8 EEA. (2010) *Agricultura Urbana y Periurbana en el Área Metropolitana de Buenos Aires*. Estacion Experimental Agropecuaria: Agropecuaria.
9 FAO. (2008) *An Introduction to the Basic Concepts of Food Security*. EC – FAO Food Security Programme: Rome.
10 FAO, OPS, WFP y UNICEF. (2019) *Panorama de la seguridad alimentaria y nutrición en América Latina y el Caribe 2019*. Santiago. 136. Licencia: CC BY-NC-SA 3.0 IGO.
11 Fernández, L. (2010) *Censo 2010. Somos 14.819.137 habitantes en la Región Metropolitana de Buenos Aires*. Universidad Nacional de General Sarmiento: Argentina.

12 Fernandez, R. (2020) *Tenemos de Terminar con el Hambre que es una Inmoralidad*. IDEP (Instituto de Estudios Sobre Estado y Participación https://canalabierto.com.ar/2020/08/14/tenemos-que-terminar-con-el-hambre-que-es-una-inmoralidad/. Accessed July 26, 2021.
13 Food and Agriculture Organization. (2012) *La Agricultura Urbana y Su Contribución a la Seguridad Alimentaria: Sistematización del Proyecto Piloto AUP en Honduras*. United Nations: Washington, DC.
14 Government of Buenos Aires. (2017) *Plan Estratégico Participativo Buenos Aires 2035*. Unidad de Coordinación del Consejo de Planeamiento Estratégico. Ciudad Autónoma de Buenos Aires: Argentina.
15 Government of Buenos Aires. (2021) *Alimentos: Datos y estadísticas* hwww.buenosaires.gob.ar/alimentos/datos-y-estadisticas. Accessed August 27, 2021.
16 Government of Buenos Aires. (2021) *Espacios Verdes*. www.buenosaires.gob.ar/laciudad/ciudad#:~:text=Los%20resultados%20definitivos%20del%20censo,las%2020%20mayores%20ciudades%20del. Accessed August 27, 2021.
17 Hoelscher, D. and Evans, A. (2012) Resource review: Child food insecurity: The economic impact on our nation, *Journal of Applied Research on Children: Informing Policy for Children at Risk*, 3: Iss. 1, Article 21.
18 Key, N. (2018) *Productivity Increases With Farm Size in the Heartland Region*. Economic Research Services – U.S. Department of Agriculture: Washington, DC.
19 Macri, M. Chain, D. and Lostri, H. (2009) *Modelo Territorial: La Ciudad Producida 2010–2060*. Secretary of Urban Development: Buenos Aires.
20 Medellin Como Vamos. (2021) *Encuesta de Percepción Ciudadana de Medellin 2021*. Medellin Como Vamos: Medellín.
21 Miranda, F., Franci, M., Delgado, M., Cuenca, V., and Quevedo, C. (2013) *Seguridad y soberanía alimentaria en Argentina*. Consejo Nacional de Investigaciones Científicas y Técnicas: Buenos Aires.
22 Ng, T. and Feldman, D. (2009) *How Broadly Does Education Contribute to Job Performance?*. Blackwell Publishing Limited: New Jersy.
23 Ordoqui, M. (2007) *Servicios de Agua Potable y Alcantarillado en la Ciudad de Buenos Aires, Argentina: Factores Determinantes de la Sustentabilidad y el Desempeño*. CEPAL. Santiago de Chile: Santiago.
24 Ortale, S. (2020) *¿Hambre Cero? Diagnóstico, perspectivas y desafíos. Ciencia, Tecnología y Política*. Universidad Nacional de La Plata: Argentina.
25 Pirez, P., Ciccolella, P., Torres, H., Merklen, D., Cravino, MC., Chiara, M., Sassone, S., Ferraudi, MC., Catenazzi, A., Gutiérrez, A., and Gorelik, A. (2009) *Buenos Aires, la formación del presente*. OLACCHI. Quito, Ecuador.
26 Prefeitura Municipal de Belo Horizonte. (1993) *Lei N° 6352, De 15 De Julho 1993. Dispõe sobre a estrutura organizacional da administração direta da Prefeitura Municipal de Belo Horizonte, e dá outras providências*. Prefeitura Municipal de Belo Horizonte: Brazil.
27 Rabin, J., Zinati, G. and Nitzsche, P. (2012) *Yield Expectations for Mixed Stand, Small-Scale Agriculture*. Rutgers New Jersey Agricultural Experiment Station. New Brunswick.
28 Rayner, G. and Lang, T. (2012) *Ecological Public Health: Reshaping the Conditions for Good Health*. Routledge: London.
29 Redacción. (2017) ¿Cómo Perú logró reducir en 10 años un 15% de la desnutrición crónica infantil? *El Comercio Peru*. https://rpp.pe/peru/actualidad/como-peru-logro-reducir-en-10-anos-un-15-de-la-desnutricion-cronica-infantil-noticia-1079200.

30 Redacción. (2018) Los 3 países con más hambre en América Latina (y el único donde aumentó en la última década). *BBC News Mundo.* www.bbc.com/mundo/noticias-45503585. Accessed August 27, 2021.
31 Rodas, M., Maldonado, A., Rodríguez, A. and Proaño, I. (2016) *Quito Siembra: Agricultura Urbana.* Quito Mayor's Office: Mayor.
32 Rodriguez, H., Santilli, D., Miguel, F., Macchiavelli, E., Morosi, R. and García, F. (2020) *Plan de Acción Climática 2050 Ciudad de Buenos Aires.* Gobierno de la Ciudad de Buenos Aires: Aires.
33 Rodriguez, J. (2004) *El Papel del Fondo Monetario Internacional en la Crisis de La Argentina.* Revista Agenda Internacional. Pontificia Universidad Católica del Perú: Perú.
34 Rosenzweig, C., Iglesius, A., Yang, XB., Epstein, P., and Chivian, E. (2001) *Climate Change and Extreme Weather Events – Implications for Food Production, Plant Diseases, and Pests.* Nasa Publications: Washington, DC.
35 Sanchez, G. (2020) *Ciudades latinoamericanas entre mediados del siglo XIX y principios del XX: del Higienismo al Urbanismo.* Universidad Autónoma Metropolitana: México.
36 Santoro, A. (2016) *Desigualdades en la Ciudad Autónoma de Buenos Aires: Mortalidad, Fecundidad y Estructura Demográfica.* Universidad Nacional de Lanús: Argentina.
37 Secretary of Interior. (2021) *La Expansión Económica.* Secretary of Interior. www.argentina.gob.ar/interior/migraciones/museo/el-estado-y-la-inmigracion/la-expansion-economica. Accessed August 27, 2021.
38 Staff Clarin. (2015) *Buenos Aires, la ciudad con más canchas de fútbol del mundo.* Diario el Clarin. ttps://www.clarin.com/ciudades/buenos-aires-ciudad-canchas-futbol_0_B1UdwVFv7x.html. Accessed August 27, 2021.
39 Tuchin, F. (2020) *La inseguridad alimentaria se agudiza en Argentina por la pandemia.* Diario el Pais. https://elpais.com/planeta-futuro/2020-11-16/la-inseguridad-alimentaria-se-agudiza-en-argentina-por-la-pandemia.html. Accessed July 26, 2021.
40 United Nations. (2013) *The State of Food Insecurity in the World.* Food and Agriculture Organization: Rome.
41 Walsh, B. and Greenwalt, J. (2022) *Findings From Innovate4Cities 2021 and Update to the Global Research and Action Agenda.* Global Covenant of Mayors for Climate & Energy (GCoM) and UN-Habitat: Washington, DC.
42 WHO. (2002) *Diet, Nutrition, and the Prevention of Chronic Diseases* (WHO technical report series). WHO: Geneva.
43 Ybran, R. and Lacelli, G. (2016) *Informe estadístico mercado de la soja.* Instituto Nacional de Tecnología Agropecuaria: Buenos Aires.

7 Medellín

(Digital) Connectivity for Social Transformation

"I'll call you later," he said to his son, then hung up the phone. He knew his calls were being traced by the police but still insisted on communicating with this family that day. He had done so several times by frequently interrupting the calls to avoid revealing his location. He was desperate. He was being hunted. After hanging up, Pablo Escobar heard the first gunshots and immediately went out the window and climbed toward the terracotta tile roof of the house that he was using as his hideout with his personal bodyguard in the Los Olivos neighborhood in the western part of Medellín. With two guns, jeans, a blue shirt, and no shoes, he crossed toward the neighbor's roof, where more shots were heard. He was hit multiple times.

Immediately after, several members of the Search Block (*Bloque de Busqueda*) – a special police squad formed by the government 16 months earlier with the sole purpose of capturing the most sought-after criminal in the world – went up the roof to confirm the capture and death of Pablo Escobar and the end of the Medellín Cartel. That day, December 2, 1993, a group of eight officers, both in uniform and civilian clothing, took a picture smiling with their weapons behind Escobar's body as a sad reminder of what was considered a prize in Colombia in the decade of the 1990s: a lifeless body.

The death of the most dangerous person in the world did not translate into peace for the country. Colombia struggled with the guerrilla groups that have been fighting the government for decades, but that became economically stronger after the dissolution of the Medellín Cartel and their entrance into the illegal drug business. It was not until September 26, 2016, that Juan Manuel Santos (then-President of Colombia) and Rodrigo Londoño, alias Timochenko, a representative of the Colombian Revolutionary Armed Forces (FARC), shook hands in a photograph that travelled around the world in a ceremony that signified a historic peace treaty with the rebel group to end a

DOI: 10.4324/9781003380818-7

50-year-old conflict and the beginning of a new era for the country. This hostility had led to hundreds of thousands of deaths, thousands of injured, disappeared, and kidnapped, and millions of people in forced displacement. This conflict pushed people to several Colombian capitals during the decades of the 1970s and 1980s. Medellín, located in a valley and the second largest city in the country, began to generate peripheral neighborhoods on its sloping edges disconnected from the formal city, just like in Lima, Buenos Aires, Bogotá, or Mexico City. Such marginalization encouraged the birth of "soldiers" of the most powerful drug cartel in the world of the 1980s and early 1990s.

By the early 2000s, after the death of Pablo Escobar and the eradication of the Medellín Cartel, the mayor's office began investing in reconnecting those neighborhoods with the rest of the city to restore a sense of visibility and belonging as the city struggled with the rediscovery of its identity and the rest of the country grappled with a shifting of the forces behind narcotraffic.[8] Through policies and urban-design interventions, the city became a world-class example of transformation (see Figure 7.1). Moreover, the concept of connectivity evolved to investing in technological advancement for the sake of preserving the goal of social transformation.[10] For more than a decade, the city has focused on economic development through investment in science, technology, and innovation (STI).

In this chapter, we will look at an overview of the development of the city and its effect on connectivity and development in Medellín. I will explain the investment efforts the city has implemented to improve its infrastructure, including its level of connectivity; I will elaborate on the importance of improving these numbers and what Medellín is doing to address social justice through technological innovation and connectivity.

Background

The city is located 422 kilometers northwest of Bogotá in the Aburrá Valley, which presents natural boundaries dissected by the Medellín River. Medellín was founded in 1616 by Spaniard Francisco de Herrera y Campuzano as San Lorenzo de Aburrá, and later, in 1675, it was integrated with a new settlement named Villa de Nuestra Señora de la Candelaria de Medellín to form what is today Medellín.

The city officially became the capital of the Department of Antioquia in 1826, shortly after the republic became independent. The department's topographical conditions protected it from

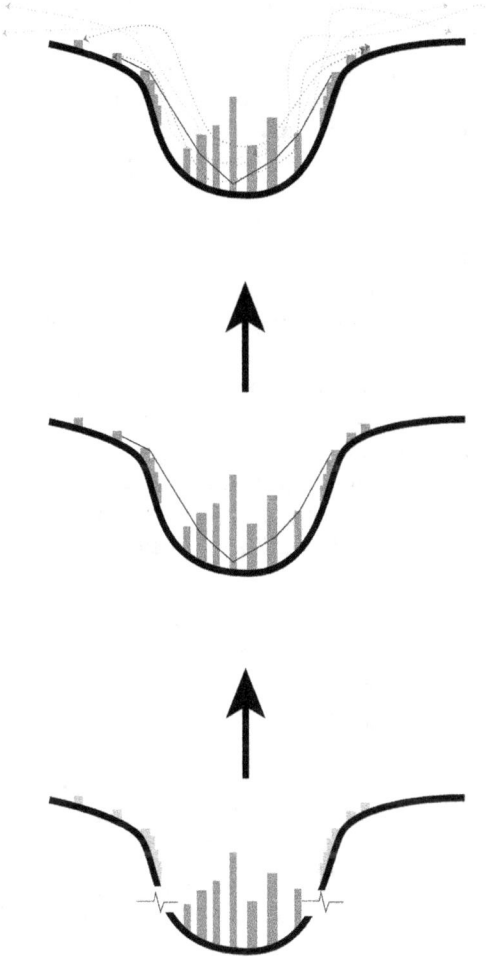

Figure 7.1 Connectivity Progress in Medellín by Camilo Espitia

the rest of the country's tribulations during the Spanish colonial times throughout the eighteenth and nineteenth centuries, and a process of internal colonization, known as "*Colonización Antioqueña*," spread families throughout the department and areas surrounding the Antioquia.

The economy of the department and the city benefited from the gold, coffee, real estate, and textile sectors' growth. The prosperity of the city and its opportunities drove thousands to its periphery to become part of its workforce and also part of the colonization process, returning to the city to grow their businesses and to access the political opportunities that Medellín offered, including better access to schools for their offspring.[21] Throughout the mid-twentieth century, large numbers of people moved toward the biggest cities in the country, and by 1951, Medellín had 358,189 people, which, compared to the 54,946 in 1905[21], meant the population grew by almost sevenfold in less than 50 years.

However, during the decade of 1970s, the city suffered a slowdown in its economy and took a hard hit in its employment numbers. The low-income people who had moved on the ladders that made up the valley suffered unemployment and segregation from society and shaped the city into what was known during the 1980s as one of the most turbulent times in the history of Colombia.

Shortly after the death of Pablo Escobar, both the public and private sectors of the city, along with civic groups, began drafting plans for the institutional and social restoration of the city, including one of the largest infrastructure projects in the history of the country: the metro rail system (see Figure 7.2). A little more than decade after,

Figure 7.2 Metrocable Medellín by Juanita Sierra

Sergio Farjardo (eventually a presidential candidate) became mayor of Medellín in 2004 and took the city on a path of social change by investing heavily in marginalized areas. This investment was focused on transportation, public facilities, education, and public spaces. Since then, subsequent mayors have prioritized the effort of public investment in the community to continue the city's evolution.

In 2013, Medellín was named the most innovative city in the world and became a symbol of urban transformation with the help of its unprecedented policies.[3] Medellín kept attracting immigrants, and according to data from the 2018 census, Medellín had a population of almost 2.5 million that year. The city is divided into 16 communes, or districts, and according to the 2018 report from the mayor's office and the Planning Administrative Department, Medellín contributes 7.45 percent of the national GDP and it is the most important city in the country, only after Bogotá in terms of productivity.[7]

Today, the current city mayor, Daniel Quintero, is an electronic engineer and software developer himself who served previously as the deputy minister of Digital Economy of Colombia as part of the Ministry of Information Technology and Communications (TIC) during the Juan Manuel Santos presidency period. His background has contributed to the support of several policies to position Medellín as a pioneer in the Latin American region and on the globe as an innovative city that strives to be connected and committed to addressing the need for technology as a tool for development.[1,2]

Internet in Colombia

The internet in Colombia began first as a fruitless attempt in 1986 with an initiative between private and public universities to connect globally to other educational institutions. That first experiment failed due to the lack of infrastructure in the country to support digital connectivity. However, it became the keystone for the National University Network of Colombia (RUNCOL), a group of universities that began to explore digital networks to connect with the rest of the world, and five years later, in 1991, Universidad del Valle in Cali, Universidad EAFIT in Medellín, and Universidad de los Andes in Bogotá succeeded in connecting with Columbia University in New York. Even though the first achievements in internet connectivity in Colombia were fostered by the educational sector, three years later, in 1994, the Colombian government, through the Department of Science, Technology, and Innovation and with the cooperation of the private and educational sectors, officially entered the global stage of the internet.[27] The signal came from a router located in Homestead, Florida, to Universidad de los Andes in Bogotá, and from there to Medellín, with a speed of 64 kb for the first time in Colombia.[29]

The efforts to connect via the internet as an economic development opportunity for the country trace back to the economic liberalization policies that began in 1990 with the government of President César Gaviria Trujillo. Despite the fact that the first attempts were educational with the intent of information exchange and research between academic institutions, the investment in the internet by the government was seen as an opportunity to invite different players in the digital-connectivity business to increase competitiveness and thus its coverage throughout the entire country. However, the educational sector was the one in charge of educating and informing the public and private sectors of the benefits of the internet and the technology necessary to stimulate its expansion.[29]

The first attempts at amplifying internet services relied on existing telephone lines that still had limited presence in the countryside and smaller cities. Unfortunately, today, the same divide is present in terms of internet connectivity; these same communities still lack connectivity, or in many cases, have lower connection speeds.[9]

As per the 2018 National Census, most of the internet coverage is in the urban nodes of the country. In Antioquia, the largest department of the country, 61 percent of urban households are connected, while only 13 percent of rural households are connected. In the Valle del Cauca department, connected urban households reach 61 percent while rural households only reach 21 percent, and in Bogotá (country capital and special district) 74 percent of urban households are connected to internet while only 20 percent of rural households have access to the service.

As an interesting note, in Medellín, even when the service is present, access to the internet is also limited in the lower "*estratos*"[5, 12, 13] due to the lack of education, understanding of the technology, and, depending on age, interest (or lack thereof) in the type of content they actually wish to inquire about and their limitations in accessing it.[25]

In terms of the Latin American region, according to the 2018 Annual Broadband Development Index Report from the Inter-American Development Bank, Chile leads the ranking of connectivity in the Latin American region, followed by Brazil, Costa Rica, Panama, and Colombia. This was measured using two parameters: (1) public policy and strategic vision, in which Colombia falls behind Chile, Brazil, Costa Rica, and Panama; and (2) infrastructure and training, which Chile also leads, with Brazil, Costa Rica, Panama, and Colombia behind.[3] This means the country as a whole has work to do to improve its connectivity.

Nevertheless, according to the 2021 Smart City Index, an international city-ranking that measures several fields of citizens' perception of their cities, Buenos Aires and Medellín lead the Latin American region in how their citizens feel about governability, services, and resources and their influence on the quality of life. This ranking is prepared by a coalition between the International Institute for Management Development and the Singapore University of Technology and Design under the perspective of what it means to be a smart city (a city that leverages digital technology as a tool for sustainable urban development) and the influence of technology on a city's operations.

In the global ranking, which is led by Singapore, Buenos Aires and Medellín are in the 98th and 101st places, respectively, followed by Mexico City, 108th; Santiago, 110th; and Bogotá, 116th. Some key attributes about this ranking include the influence of technology in areas such as health and safety, mobility, general activities, work and school, and governance. Medellín leads in online access to job listings that make it easier to find work or the ability to process identification documents online resulting in reduced waiting times, or the online scheduling and ticket sales that have made public transportation easier to use. These results highlight the efforts Medellín has gone through to digitally connect the community to improve their quality of life.

The Colombian Congress passed Law 2108 in July 2021, also known as the Law of the Internet, as an essential and universal public service. The law aims at reducing the digital divide in the country and increasing development, especially in rural areas.

Importance of Connectivity in Medellín

As mentioned earlier, disconnectedness was an issue for many residents in the city before the internet era. What contributed to some of the most painful memories in the history of Colombia during the Cartel Wars was the fracture between a city with access to opportunities and one without the possibility of a future for many disenfranchised residents on the hills of the city. Connectivity in Medellín led to its rebirth. Connectivity in Medellín generates economic and social development by attracting tourism and patron visits to businesses, as well as facilitating transportation to employment and education centers.

Simultaneously, digital connectivity is the key to the city's future. Devoting effort to reducing the negative impact of the digital divide in Medellín is key to social equity. Digital connectivity also contributes to transparency through e-governance, allowing individuals to assess accountability from the government and at the same time participate in the policymaking process. This can translate into cost savings for municipal spending by digitizing paperwork and records, permitting processes, and payment obligations. Connectivity also contributes to the spread of culture and the sharing of knowledge, saving of time and energy consumption by reducing travel from traditional, physical errands and meetings.

However, there is a further way in which the internet has been vital for today's society. During the COVID-19 pandemic, the world had to rely on internet connectivity for essential medical needs and critical life-saving information, vaccination, social distancing, and other vital data.[26] This was critical in Medellín during the pandemic because the isolation measures did not show positive results inasmuch as people still needed to buy groceries or access public services and work, which contributed to the spread of the virus during 2021.[18]

Bringing the citizenry together and connecting them to services and opportunities through the use of technology is a way to build social resiliency and increase the quality of life.

Addressing the Digital Divide

The digital divide is the unequal advantage of access to equipment, connectivity, or literacy to access the internet. Today, digital connectivity is part of how citizens operate to network and forge bonds that build social capital today and in the future. That is why, for urban planners, digital systems and tools are important to planning for public spaces and other types of connectivity infrastructure, as discussed in the Bogotá chapter. The conglomeration of innovation hubs in certain areas of the city through zoning ordinances help to foster digital entrepreneurship, while the inclusion of Wi-Fi connections in public spaces and buildings are strategies urban planners can use to decrease the digital divide. City planning should also include funding for infrastructure, education, and the incorporation of technology in some services, such as public transportation and open spaces.

"The access to digital connectivity" refers not only to coverage and the availability of Wi-Fi connection. It also refers to the access to adequate equipment to acquire connectivity and the knowledge and skills to use such equipment. In fact, in 2016, the UN declared access to the internet as a basic human right because access to the internet is beyond leisure or entertainment. It is a utility that helps people connect to information, education, health care, and jobs. In Medellín, for example, a 2020 study by Ruta N, a private-public venture to develop, promote, and operate activities of science, technology, innovation, and entrepreneurship to support economic development as part of their implement-Smart-City projects, showed that the lowest income households pay, on average, more of their income than the highest income households to have internet at home.[23]

Digital connectivity is also important for economic development because it contributes to entrepreneurial capacity and supports the overall economic growth of a region. When a nation strengthens its digital connectivity, its economy grows, improving its GDP and its economic competency in different markets.[22] It also contributes to job creation and income increase[11] by connecting users to job opportunities and giving them the ability to work remotely once hired. Digital connectivity contributes to cities' competitiveness in that it expands their economic development opportunities so they don't have to solely rely on the physical environment. It also allows cities to immerse themselves in the global market and expand their range of resources and partnerships with either con-national or international cities and both the public and private sectors.

According to the 2016 World Bank Connectivity Report, the ICT (internet communication technology) sector enables jobs at around 3–5 percent in OECD countries (Organization for Economic Co-operation and Development) and almost 2 percent in Colombia. This is because nowadays, these types of technologies increase opportunities to find jobs while encouraging social inclusion in different sectors of the population, including people with disabilities. The ICT sector also allows for social and economic connectivity between the city and the rural sector, which has implications on food production, distribution, costs, and availability. Digital connectivity also has effects on governance transparency and, as more informational and data processes become digitized, access to internet connectivity is important to accessing social services and doing routine errands such as paying bills, applications, and notarial services.

Unfortunately, despite the growth of users of technology in Latin America, the infrastructure in the region is falling behind. During the 2020 pandemic, connectivity for economic development became an evident factor in the prosperity of Medellín as businesses without an online presence suffered the most. However, it also became an opportunity to implement mitigation strategies such as the creation of a geo-localized information system to provide money and food for those in need during the quarantine. There were also programs, such as employee biosafety registration, to allow and control the numbers of people who could go to work.

In order for Medellín to be competitive in the global market and increase service coverage for its residents, the city needs to make sure the broadband coverage improves, infrastructure investment increases, and policies strengthen education and access to technology.

How Has Medellín Invested in Digital Connectivity?

Public investment in Colombia is managed by the National Planning Department (DNP) through the Finance and Public Investment Administration (DFIP). The DFIP verifies that public investment is done in a way that aligns with the National Development Plan and prepares the Annual Operational Investment Plan for review and approval by the National Council for Economic and Social Planning (CONPES).

Until 2011, national revenue was mainly distributed back in the areas where oil drilling and mining took place. However, starting in 2014, the focus of redistribution of revenue shifted to fund projects that generate impact at a regional level, especially to support social, economic, and environmental improvements, including technology and projects that contribute to the peace-building policies that began in 2012.[6] Antioquia, with one of the largest areas and populations in the country, received the largest amount of investment from the national revenue system.[15]

A balanced public expenditure is key to a sustainable development and to Medellín's ability to focus spending on the right sectors and the right locations to guarantee that the entire population reaps equal benefits from the municipal investment. In 2022, the Mayor's Office of Medellín projected more than $319,000 million ($68.5 million USD) for the years 2023 and 2024, to improve the infrastructure of 301 educational institutions in the 16 communes (see Table 7.1). Most of the investment is intended for low-income areas. Medellín is subdivided into 16 districts, called *comunas* (communes) with predominant "*estratos*," as explained in the Bogota chapter.

According to the Medellin Council Office, some of the challenges in consolidating Medellín as a smart city include the constant change in leadership, lack of stakeholder alignment, lack of a clear plan, and the lack of understanding the need for a shift in mentality and culture to support this transformation. Nevertheless, in 2010, the city founded Ruta N, to improve the quality of life of the inhabitants of the city through science, technology, and innovation. It is based on a

Table 7.1 by Camilo Espitia, Based on Information by the Mayor's Office of Medellín

Medellin Investment in School Infrastructure

Commune	Number of Schools Investment	Predominant Estratos
Villa Hermosa	31	2
Manrique	28	2
Doce de Octubre	28	2
Aranjuez	25	3
Robledo	24	2
Castilla	23	3
Santa Cruz	22	2
Belen	22	2
Popular	21	2
San Javier	19	2
Buenos Aires	16	3
La America	12	4
Guayabal	11	3
La Candelaria	10	4
Laureles	6	5
El Polado	3	6
Total	**301**	–

world-category ecosystem by leading an economic evolution toward activities in the fields of science, technology, and innovation in an inclusive and sustainable manner.[24]

In 2012, Medellín passed a 10-year plan for science, technology, and innovation with the vision of increasing productivity capacity in the areas of knowledge, lowering unemployment levels, raising the monthly income per capita, improving the educational standards of local higher-education institutions, incrementally increasing the percentage of GPD invested in STI (science, technology, and innovation), expanding health services quality and coverage, and implementing energy-smart grids, among other goals.

In the past decade, this plan has increased the execution of its programs through acquiring funding and encouraging coordination with several of the stakeholders, increasing competitiveness and economic development.[30]

At the same time, the city launched Law 1712 on Transparency and Access to Public Information in 2014 to publish big data on infrastructure, surveys, and education, as well as to facilitate e-governance and allow citizens to run errands on the internet.[19] A year later, in 2015, the city created the Secretary of Economic Development, which later triggered the creation of the Secretary of Digital Innovation. As of 2018, public investment in science, technology, and innovation (STI) was 2.27 percent of its GDP and 1.24 percent in research and development (R&D), according to Colombian Observatory of Science and Technology. However, even though this means an improvement, in contrast with previous levels of investment, it still falls behind compared to other economies, such as the 4.3 percent of the GDP that South Korea spent for research and development. This has implications for shared knowledge and productivity numbers. Another challenge found in the technology sector in Medellín is inequity of access in relationship to expenditure: people with higher incomes spend less for internet access than those with lower incomes. Three years later, in 2018, Medellín was the city with the greatest free internet coverage in Colombia, offering free Internet connection in 237 public spaces, including parks, pocket parks, public sports facilities, and metro stations (see Figure 7.3).[31]

In January 2022, Daniel Quintero, Medellín's mayor, announced a pilot to implement free internet to the entire city.[14] The pilot began with free internet to 20 households in the San Sebastián de Palmitas

Figure 7.3 Free Public Wi-Fi by Alexander Canas Arango
Source: Shutterstock.

rural neighborhood and the installation of a public Wi-Fi zone in the village of Urquitá, the neighborhood with the lowest connectivity index in the Medellín metropolitan region.[14] The pilot also includes free internet for six months for 500 families in the Salado neighborhood in Commune 13, one of the most historically dangerous communes in the city.[16]

The city's efforts toward social-equity policies are not only visible in the investment of its people and its physical infrastructure, but also in its virtual framework to guarantee an open-ended conversation and distribution of data[17] for a more transparent execution of its programs in its current and previous administrations. The city created innovation and data centers as joint ventures between the public and the private sectors that provided increased connectivity, e-governance, and more access to data. These high-tech incubators are designed to provide regulatory mechanisms to spur innovation while, at the same time, serving as spaces that offer equipment and setups that contribute to coworking, networking, and educational programs. This, in turn, provided the city with crucial tools to move Medellín toward becoming a smarter city. Medellín is implementing Software Valley Centers (*Centros del Valle del Software*), which are innovation hubs for technology and entrepreneurial support and training with the goal of opening 21 centers throughout the city through 2023.

Medellín in the Future

The goals that Medellín has established for itself in the future are aligned with the efforts from the past decade to strengthen the access to technology for its citizens. For that reason, Ruta N has established a series of focus areas that include sustainability, education and employment, security, and health, for which science, technology, and innovation (STI) would serve as the tools to address those areas. Because the purpose is to improve the quality of life of the citizens by engaging in initiatives around technology and innovation, the city wants to increase the investment in STI to reach 7 percent of the national GDP and 3.5 percent in research and development (R&D).

The *Plan de Desarrollo Medellín Futuro 2020–2023* aims at providing 100 percent of households with an internet connection. Medellín is also implementing "*Distrito F*," an urban technology sandbox to increase and facilitate access to high-speed internet, data acquisition, and sharing-smart platforms. The sandbox also aims to implement strategies to promote the productive use of the internet; stimulate entrepreneurial frameworks to bring together the educational sector, incubators, and investors; create and expose business models that foster the use of technology for education; and formulate policies for digital technology.

At the same time, "*Distrito F*" is promoting a 5G pilot in coordination with the mayor's office, the business community, and public health and educational institutions to address issues of smart mobility, virtual medical care, and education access.

By 2030, Medellín's vision is to improve lives of its citizens through the productive and ethical use of data and through the adoption of the Fourth Industrial Revolution technologies to be in the top three smart cities in Latin America. Part of the actual implementation for reaching the goal of connectivity is the development of a neutral fiber-optics network throughout the city, which increases the speed and quality of connectivity.

Medellín's transformation in the past two decades serves as a strong foundation for the years to come where data and technology will be fundamental for the city to keep providing its citizens with the tools and opportunities for change. In the immediate future, the quality of life of citizens will be linked to how technology is handled by the government. However, for the city, advancing digital connectivity is an investment in its own administration. As Anthony Townsend states in his book *Smart Cities: Big Data, Civic Hackers, and the Quest for a New Utopia*, while offering connectivity for its citizens is a matter of social justice, the city itself benefits from cost savings and an increase in operations efficiency.[28]

Citizen participation and connectivity between the people and the government will help cities provide better services with better timing, better resource management, and more sustainable mechanisms. Medellín is on the right track to become a smart city at a global scale. In 2017, the city ranked fourth-smartest city in Latin America, only behind Buenos Aires, Santiago de Chile, and Mexico City. Meanwhile, its global ranking is 96th.[20] As of last year, it is the most connected city in Colombia with 197 free internet spots throughout the city.

Smart cities provide the indispensable trait of connectivity. The capacity of the citizenry to participate in the decision-making process of cities is critical for the sustainable growth of cities. Citizens not only build the city with their behavior and interactions with each other and the built environment but also through the symbiotic relationship with the government. Technology and big data can become the door between the city and its citizens. Urban activist Jane Jacobs once said that cities can provide services for all citizens when the city is created by everyone.[4]

Public engagement in city planning during pre-pandemic times was heavily reliant on the physical presence of residents in a single room – an inconvenience for those with kids at home, attending school, or at work. This meant granting participation and decision-making to only a few. Since the pandemic, the use of technology has been crucial to getting community feedback, as it presents the opportunity to expand engagement by including a wider sector of the population with diverse age groups, languages, nationalities, proximity to meetings, accessibility challenges, public-speaking limitations, or the mere availability to attend a single forum. However, technology access and literacy are essential for the outreach to be true and participation to be meaningful and create an impact.

Connectivity is essential to a city that wants to become a just city, and for Medellín, it was the fundamental tool for transformation. Medellín in the future needs to keep working on its digital connectivity and expand it beyond email access, online shopping, or social media. Digital connectivity is a matter of equity as Medellín keeps evolving to thrive and prosper. People in Medellín need to connect to the internet and to others, but most importantly, to their own sense of place and ownership of the city.

References

1 Alvarez, A. (2015) Medellín, la ciudad de mayor inversión pública. *El Colombiano*. www.elcolombiano.com/antioquia/medellin-la-ciudad-de-mayor-inversion-publica-EX2202611. Accessed April 24, 2018.
2 Alvarez, A. (2017) Presupuesto de Medellín para inversión: ¿qué tan social es?. *El Colombiano*. www.elcolombiano.com/antioquia/alcaldia-de-medellin-dice-que-2-6-billones-de-su-presupuesto-apuntan-a-lo-social-NB5762681. Accessed April 22, 2018.
3 BBC Staff. (2013) Colombia's Medellin Named 'Most Innovative City'. *BBC*. www.bbc.com/news/world-latin-america-21638308. Accessed Apr 22, 2018.
4 Center for the Living City. (2018) *Jane Jacobs and the Center*. http://centerforthelivingcity.org/janejacobs. Accessed Apr 22, 2018.
5 Colombian Congress. (1994) *Law 142 of 1994 on Domiciliary Public Services*. Bogota. Government of Colombia.
6 Colombian Congress. (2014) *Law 1712 of March 6th 2014 on Transparency and Access to Public Information*. Bogota. Government of Colombia.
7 DANE. (2018) *Producto Interno Bruto. Departamento Administrativo de Planeacion*. DANE: Alcalde de Medellin.
8 Digital Colombian Government. (2018) *Datos Abiertos*. www.datos.gov.co. Accessed Apr 19, 2018.
9 Erb, S. (2019) *Colombia is becoming an online country, but a digital divide still separates cities from the countryside*. Deutsche Welle: Germany. www.

dw.com/en/colombia-is-becoming-an-online-country-but-a-digital-divide-still-separates-cities-from-the-countryside/a-47563079. Accessed March 22, 2022.
10. Garcia, A. and Iglesias, E. (2018) *Annual Broadband Development Index Report*. Inter-American Development Bank: Washington, DC.
11. Garcia, A. and Iglesias, E. (2018) *Cloud Computing: Opportunities and Challenges for Social Economic Development in Latin America and the Caribbean*. Inter-American Development Bank: Washington, DC.
12. Health Department of Colombia. (2018) *Régimen Subsidiado*. www.minsalud.gov.co/salud/Paginas/RégimenSubsidiado.aspx. Accessed April 20, 2018.
13. IEEE Smart Cities. (2018) *IEEE Affiliated Smart City Profile – Medellín, Colombia*. https://smartcities.ieee.org/affiliated-cities/medellin-colombia.html. Accessed April 19, 2018.
14. Infobae. (2022) Inician piloto para llevar internet gratis a los hogares de Medellín. www.infobae.com/america/colombia/2022/01/22/inician-piloto-para-llevar-internet-gratis-a-los-hogares-de-medellin/. Accessed March 22, 2022.
15. Lauletta. (2019) *Monitoreando la inversión pública El impacto de MapaRegalías en Colombia*. Inter-American Development Bank: Washington, DC.
16. Lopera, E. (2021) En Medellín 500 hogares del barrio El Salado tendrán internet gratis y de alta velocidad. *ElMetro.com*. https://elmetro.com.co/en-medellin-500-hogares-del-barrio-el-salado-tendran-internet-gratis-y-de-alta-velocidad/#ixzz7OszZUiFF. Accessed March 22, 2022.
17. Mayer-Schöenberger, V. and Cukier, K. (2014) *Big Data*. Houghton Mifflin Harcourt: New York.
18. Medellin Como Vamos. (2021) *Situación del Covid-19 en Medellin y el Valle de Aburra*. www.medellincomovamos.org/situacion-covid-19-medellin-y-valle-de-aburra. Medellin Como Vamos. Accessed March 22, 2022.
19. Medellin Mayor's Office. (2018) *Virtual Window*. www.medellin.gov.co/irj/portal/medellin/ventanilla. Accessed April 16, 2018.
20. Ossa, G. (2017) Medellín, cuarta ciudad más inteligente de Latinoamérica según estudio. *El Tiempo*. www.eltiempo.com/colombia/medellin/medellin-cuarta-ciudad-mas-inteligente-de-latinoamerica-segun-estudio-98360. Accessed April 21, 2018.
21. Ramirez, S. (2011) *Cuando Antioquia se volvió Medellín, 1905–1950. Los perfiles de la inmigración pueblerina hacia Medellín*. Universidad de Antioquia: Medellín.
22. Revinova, S. and Chavarry, D. (2020) *E-Government and Government Support for the Digital Economy in Latin America and the Caribbean*. Peoples' Friendship University of Russia (RUDN University), Mikluho-Maklaya Str,6, Moscow, 117198, Russia.
23. Ruta, N. (2018) *Ruta N Medellin: Business and Innovation Center*. www.rutanmedellin.org/es/actualidad/noticias/tag/Big%20Data. Accessed April 17, 2018.
24. Ruta, N. (2018) *Ruta N Medellin: Business and Innovation Center*. www.rutanmedellin.org/es/nosotros/ruta-n/sobre-nosotros. Accessed April 17, 2018.
25. Sanchez, J. and Florez, C. (2014) *Causas Para la Falta de Interes en Acceder a Internet en los Estratos 1 Y 2 en la Estación Metro Acevedo de la Ciudad de Medellín*. Universidad Santo Tomas: Medellin.

26 Sanders, C. and Scanlon, E. (2020) *The Digital Divide Is a Human Rights Issue: Advancing Social Inclusion Through Social Work Advocacy.* Journal of Human Rights and Social Work. Springer, Nature: Geneva.
27 Tamayo, C., Delgado, J., and Penagos, J. (2008) *Génesis del campo de Internet en Colombia: elaboración estatal de las relaciones informacionales. Signo y Pensamiento.*
28 Townsend, A. (2014) *Smart Cities: Big Data, Civic Hackers, and the Quest for a New Utopia.* W.W. Norton: London.
29 Universidad de los Andes. (2018) *El salto hacia el ciberespacio* https://uniandes.edu.co/es/noticias/ingenieria/el-salto-hacia-el-ciberespacio. Universidad de los Andes: Bogota.
30 Valdes, A., García, C., Bedoya, I.. and Roldán, P. (2020) *Medellin: Una Ciudad que Avanza a Traves de Políticas Públicas de Ciencia, Tecnologia, e Innovation.* Unidad de Política Pública Ruta N. Medellín, Colombia.
31 www.caracol.com.co. (2018) *Medellín es la ciudad con mayor conexión a internet gratis en Colombia.* https://caracol.com.co/emisora/2018/03/02/medellin/1519998451_846360.html. Accessed June 16, 2019.

8 The Future

From 6th to 8th grade, I attended a public school in Bogotá that charged tuition based on household income. Even though I was lucky enough to not have to endure the struggles that my parents, grandparents, or some of my classmates did, their experiences became the motivation to undertake this study for the sake of future generations. As I have worked on projects in the region and as a planner who constantly engages with immigrant, underrepresented communities, my commitment is to plan for cities that are welcoming, kind, and just.

The concept of the ideal city varies from person to person; however, a just city should provide the tools to make choices without being detrimental to the environment or at the cost of increasing the equity gap that already exists, especially in Latin American cities.

A just city is where rights, responsibilities, and their consequences are equally spread out. This ability to understand the city as a collective place that belongs to all is part of what defines the community, even with their vast differences. Part of how cities formed in the first place was because people began to understand their surroundings as part of their identity.[5]

Plato considered social justice a virtue; a moral choice made by people to live in harmony with others.[3] However, social justice ought not to be a choice but rather a community's obligation to every individual because it benefits everyone. City planning should provide the opportunities to participate, contribute, cooperate, and enjoy the benefits of the community.

Urban planning for social justice provides access to mechanisms for wealth creation such as employment, education, and social mobility. It also addresses mental and physical health through environmental justice. However, city planning also entails the abstract concept of sense of belonging because a just society sees the individual as an equal and not as the other.

DOI: 10.4324/9781003380818-8

Around the globe, other cities have attempted to solve similar issues. New Delhi, similar to Lima, also suffers pollution from transportation and particles that come from unpaved roads. This city also installed several air-quality sensors around the city, identifying hotspots, and attempting to reduce emissions from traffic. One of its policies from 1998 was to change all public transportation fuel from gas to compressed natural gas (CNG).[2] Cape Town in South Africa, comparable to Mexico City and its water supply challenges, avoided Day Zero (a day of finally shutting faucets off due to lack of water) by implementing campaigns to change behavior and a thorough analysis if its supply- and demand-management practices.[1]

What is critical about the Latin American region is that it is projected that the majority of the population will live in cities and that more than 77 percent of Latin Americans lack safe sanitation due to poor infrastructure.[4] City planning in this region is essential for social justice and their proximity to one another, their common development trends, language, geopolitical similitudes, and trade agreements are advantages that should be leveraged to forge a strong network of cities.

This book is conveyed through the possibilities that these cities have forged for themselves by addressing urban-planning strategies that transcend financial resources and political power. They unfold from the commitment of years of planning, acknowledging the issues, including the community in the planning process, and deliberately planning for resiliency. Understanding the context under which the region operates is important because it helps to illustrate the enormity of their efforts to achieve what they have achieved. With limited budgets and generations of recalcitrant political mechanisms, the wealth of talent in the area has had to multiply their efforts to ensure the narrative of success and implementation. At present, the resilient Latin American city is being developed, but the story is not being told.

In 2021, Bogotá approved the "Bogotá Cundinamarca Metropolitan Region Law" to implement a regional master plan that protects regional environmental assets and develops bold mobility projects; Mexico City is investing in infrastructure that collects, treats, and recycles water to improve coverage and quality supply to the entire city; Lima is investing in its public transportation system to reduce pollution; Santiago is implementing policies that help reduce energy consumption and move on to sustainable energy sources; Buenos Aires is integrating a series of initiatives to reduce food insecurity in its master-plan implementation with specific goals and measures to gauge progress; and Medellín is heavily invested in addressing its digital divide by investing in infrastructure, coverage, and education to increase connectivity and prosperity for all its citizens.

The Cost of Solving Problems Now vs Tomorrow

Nonetheless, these efforts come at a cost. Financial resources are limited and the decisions to prioritize investments have to be made while the relentlessness of time hovers over the future of these cities. With limited resources, planning for resiliency is key not only to resolving the issues of today but also to delineating the trajectory moving forward while allowing flexibility for the unpredictable future. Defining who they are today and who they want to be in the future is important in outlining the steps toward thriving today without sacrificing their own sources for the coming generations.

City planners in the region have demonstrated the capacity to establish development goals in congruity with their own social, cultural, economic, historic, geographical, and environmental contexts. These case studies have come to terms with the tradeoffs that help forge their identity. However, intensifying these practices and taking advantage of the ability to replicate the efforts of other cities in the region, adapting them to their specific conditions, will help these cities to respond, adapt, and recuperate from events that will come in the future. An economically resilient city can better respond to the market's fluctuations; socially resiliency helps foster the sense of community and diversity, social exchange and connections; while an environmentally resilient city can better respond to climate threats such as rising sea levels or global warming.

However, cities should not only strive to find ways to only respond to environmental, economic, or social changes, but should look for ways to evolve with these transformations. In other words, rather than only considering how to reduce their impact in the present or how to mitigate the shocks of the future, cities should grow with their contexts and develop adaptation mechanisms that allow for a constant change to reduce the negative impact of the unknown.

Environmental, social, and economic resiliency in these Latin American cities starts by their understanding the context and transforming their communities by adapting to their local characteristics and allowing natural processes to be part of their urban development. These cities' case studies target resiliency while addressing social justice, and the ideas described here are an indicator of the possibility of change and success for a region with common trends of development. Hopefully, this book shows that change is possible in any community and that we can develop just, kind, welcoming, equitable cities.

References

1. Joubert, L. and Ziervogel, G. (2019) *Day Zero. One City's Response to a Record-Breaking Drought.* Tandym Print: Cape Town.
2. Kumar, P., Mukesh, K., Harrison, R., Bloss, W., Alastair, L., Coe, H., and Morawska, L. (2015) *New Directions: Air Pollution Challenges for Developing Megacities Like Delhi.* Department of Civil and Environmental Engineering, Faculty of Engineering and Physical Sciences (FEPS). University of Surrey: Guildford.
3. LeBar, M. (Fall 2020 Edition). Justice as a virtue. In *The Stanford Encyclopedia of Philosophy*, Edward N. Zalta (ed.). Stanford University: Stanford.
4. Muggah, R. (2018) Latin America's Cities are Ready to Take off. But their Infrastructure is Failing them. *World Economic Forum.* www.weforum.org/agenda/2018/06/latin-america-cities-urbanization-infrastructure-failing-robert-muggah. Accessed July 24, 2020.
5. Newitz, A. (2021) *Four Lost Cities* (1st ed.). W. W. Norton & Company: New York City.

Index

Note: Page locators in **bold** indicate a table. Page locators in *italics* indicate a figure.

access: to clean water 31, 38, 42, 57; to digital connectivity 119–120; to education 19–21, 126; to employment 12, 14; to food 7, 59, 92, 96, 105, 110 (*see also* food security); to transportation 17, 64
acknowledge/acknowledgment 3, 5, 76, 105, 131
adapt/adaptability 3–5, 80, 132
Africa 13, 101, 131
agriculture: challenges 107, 109 (*see also* urban agriculture); land use 26, 92
air pollution 50, 52, 55, 59
air quality: diminished 6, 47, 59; improvements 66; Lima 46, 51–52; monitoring stations 56; sensor, use of 55–56, 60, 66, 131
air quality: decontamination process 61
Allende, Salvador 72
aquifers 31–32, 34, 38–39
architect 1, 20
Area de Emisiones Reducidas (AER) 60
Argentina: air quality 58; demographics 92–93; economic policies 13; exports 91; food distribution 96–98, 100–101; GDP/credit financing 63

Atlantic Council Adrianne Arsht Latin American Center 13
Aztecs 32

Baena, Andrea 20
banks 11, 17, 91, 101; *see also* financial institutions
Beitler, Ady 101
belonging 2, 10, 27, 114, 130
Bernal, Diana Maria Morneo 19
bicycle lane 5, 18, 24, 26, 54, 64, 84
biodiversity 42, 98
biofuel 79
Bogotá: education access 20; land structure 14, *15–16*, 17; social mobility 8–9, 18, 21; *see also* Colombia
Bogotá Educational Institutions Master Plan 20
Bogotá River 17
Bogotá Secretary of Education 20
Bogotá Secretary of Planning 18, 20
Bogotá Social Mobility Index Bulletin 18, **19**, 21
Brazil 63, 87, 118–119
British Empire 95
bronchitis 57
Buenos Aires: demographics 50, 95–96; food production 6, 13, 91, 97, 100 (*see also* food security);

food waste 101–102; foundations 93, *94*; health system 102–104
built environment: economic conditions and 18, 20–21, 96, 126; social community 2, 8–9, 11, 23

Callao Port 66–67
canals 34, 47–48
capacity: food production 96–97, 105, 110; zoning 6, 12
cardiac disease 50, 57, 79
casas chorizo 95
case studies 4, 6–7, 132
Castelar, George 60
CCS (carbon capture and storage) 82
CDC (Centers for Disease Control) 102
challenges: agricultural 92, 107; air quality improvement 60, 63; economic 10, 13, 105; transportation 64; waste management 36, 51
change: ecological 3–4, 36 (*see also* climate change); social 41, 43, 117, 132
children: education of 12, 17–20; health and welfare 63, 100, 104; low-income 24
Chile 5, 19, 48, 58; *see also* Santiago
Chilean Agency of Energy Efficiency (ACHEE) 76
China 10, 80
Ciclovia 23
citizen participation 37, 68, 126
City of Kings 48
city planning: planners 4, 11, 49, 105, 110, 120, 130; potential 3–4, 27, 50
clean air 4, 62, 79
Clean and Sustainable Region 84
clean energy 61, 67, 80, 82, 84
climate change 34, 80, 87, 109; *see also* global warming
coal 72–73, 77, 79–80
Colombia: digital networks 117–119 (*see also* Medellin); estrato 14, 18; GDP 63; homeownership 22, 37; land structure 14 (*see also* Bogotá); poor social mobility 19–20; violence 8, 46, 113–114, 116

Colombian Observatory of Science and Technology 124
colonial times 1, 93, 95, 115
colonization/colonizers 32, 48, 74, 115–116
commerce 22, 50, 77
community: centers 11, 51, 65; engagement 21, 84, 105; greenhouses 98, 106–107; kitchens 92, 100; productivity 13, 26, 37
connection 36, 59, 74, 96
connectivity 118, 120, 124–125
Consultive Water Council of Mexico 38
Costa Rica 118–119
COVID-19: impact 57, 61; quarantine 5, 57–58, 61, 74, 100, 121
cultural: capital 11, 22, 24, 83; resources 27, 62
Curitiba 5
currency 13, 72, 91
Cusco 1, 109

density: of development 14, *15*, 17, 36, 64, 82; population 58, 61
development: economic 49, 61, 93, 107, 121; mixed-use 12, 14, 17, 22, 27, 64, 82; urban 4, 6, 66, 81–82, 92, 119, 132
digital connectivity *see* connectivity
diverse/diversity 27, 43, 127, 132

Ecological Public Health 102–103
economic: development 49, 61, 93, 107, 121; prosperity 49–50, 73, 80
Economic Commission for Latin America and the Caribbean (ECLAC) 63
education: access to 19–20, 126; dropout rate 19
electricity: consumption 74, 77, 81; expansion of 49, 72–73
employment: centers 10–12, 14, 50; generation of 42, 107, 116, 125, 130; status 18, 21, **23**, 26
energy: burden 81; efficiency 5, 72, 76, 79, 84, 86–87; renewable 66, 79, 80, 84, 86, 98; tax 82, 87

energy consumption: efficiency of production 79; initiatives 81–85; metropolitan Santiago 76, **78**, 81; uncontrolled 80–81, 86
Energy Sustainability Agency (ESA) 84
environment: natural 49, 104; *see also* built environment
environmental justice 35, 46, 57, 68, 92, 130
Environmental Protection Agency 98
equity 2, 12, 17, 27, **35**, 127, 130; *see also* social equity
estrato 18, **19**, 21

financial institutions 22, 91
food: resources 96, 107; security 91–93, 97, 101–102, 105, 109; waste 101, 108
Food and Agriculture Organization (FAO) 98, 101
formal: city 22, 114; employment 26; investment 17
fossil fuels 52, 55, 58, 79–80
future responsibility 130

Gaitán, Jorge Eliecer 8
gasoline 72
global: economic crisis 72, 75; gross domestic product (GDP) 12; perception 4; warming 80, 108, 132; *see also* climate change
Global North 5
Great Depression 75
green open space 14, 49–51, 109
greenhouse gas emissions (GHG) 66, 78, 86–87
growth: economic 26, 68, 75, 80, 86, 121; population 5, 32, 36, 40, 48, 95, 105

health: biomedical 103; public 33, 73, 102–104, 126, 4866; techno-economic 103
high-speed rail 36; *see also* transportation
Hoelscher, Deanna 104
homeownership 12, 22, **23**
hope 3
hostile/hostility 4, 114

housing 5; affordability 11–12, 14, 22, 63, 79; mixed-use development 14, 22, 27, 64–65, 82
housing, low-cost 20–21, 60
Humboldt, Alexander von 1
hunger 6, 98, 100–101, 109
Hunger Fighter Map 100
hydroelectric plants 73, 78–79, 87

IDA (International Development Association) 37
identity 2, 47, 114, 130, 132
implement/implementation: air quality measures 60–61; internet for all 124–125; policy 36, 63, 107; public transit 26, 54
Inca Empire 1, 47–48, 74, 109
inclusive 3, 68, 88, 109, 123
independence 1, 74, 93
India 80
industrial: production 50, 55; revolution 109, 126; sectors 50, 58, 75, 77, 80
inequality 5, 13, 37, 75, 81, 96–97
inflation 47, 72, 107
influence 2, 11, 13, 67, 119
informality 14, 21, 51–52
infrastructure: aging 37–38; financing 37; improvement 67; urban 17, 20, 49, 62
initiatives 3, 59, 63–64, 81, 125, 131
innovation 5, 84, 114, 120–123
inspire/inspiration 4–5
Inter-American Development Bank 22–23, 118
Intergenerational Social Mobility in Latin America 19
International Monetary Fund **63**
International Monetary Fund (IMF) 91
Internet 117; *see also* connectivity
internet communication technology (ICT) 121
interviews 4–5
investment: financial 37, **63**, 91; infrastructure 1, 11, **35**, 95, 108, 122; real estate 10
invisible 3

Index

kindness 2
knowledge sharing 6, 98, 103, 120, 124

land: preservation 17, 47; structure 9, 14, 96; use 2, 6, 21, 48–50, 62, 92, 105
land use 50–52
Lang, Tim 102
La Plata River 96
Laws of the Indies 1, 74
Lima Metropolitan Development Plan 62
Lima-Callao Plan of Action for Air Qualtiy Improvement 61
Lima, Peru: air quality 55; pedestrian safety 64; terrorism 46
Lincoln Institute of Land Policy 66
livability 3, 40, 67, 103

malnutrition 102, 104–105
Mapocho River 74
marginalization 2, 114
mass transit 65
Mazumdar, Soumya 11
Medellín: citizen participation 68, 100; city center 7, 116–117; connectivity 113, *115*, 119–120, 122; digital divide 120, 122; future of 126; school infrastructure **123**
Medellín River 114
metropolitan area 50, **51**
Mexico City: challenges 32–33, 40; earthquake 31–32, 38–39; infrastructure 34, **35**, 38–39; water supply/management 32, 37–38, 40, 43
Mexico City Water Systems Agency (SACMEX) 37
migration 6, 10–11, 49, 59, 93, 95
Milan Urban Food Policy Pact 98
Milder, Jody 36
Ministry of Information Technology and Communications (TIC) 117
mobility 34, 42, 84; *see also* social mobility
mortality 57, 79, 96

NASA 67
National Association of Financial Institutions (ANIF) 22
National Plan for Food Security (PNSA) 91
natural environment 49, 104
neighborhood: quality 14, 21–22, **23**; urban 64–65, 83, 98, 114, 125; wealthy 51
nitrogen dioxide (NO2) 55–56, 58, 79

Obrecht, Raúl 80
OECD (Organisation for Economic Co-operation and Development) 12, 121
oil crisis 72
opportunities: economic 5, 10, 12, 22, 50; employment 14, 22, 104
ozone (O) 55

Pacific War 75
Palacios, Javier 72
Panama 87, 118–119
parks 2, 11–12, 22, 60, 106, 124
participation: community **23**, 62, 98, 100; private PPIs 37; public 21, 38, 68, 76, 86
particulate matter (PM) 55, 61
partnerships 41, 121
Peron, Juan Domingo 96
Peruvian National System of Environmental Information (SINIA) 50
PESTEL 34, **35**
Pinochet, Augusto 75
Pizarro, Francisco 47
planners (city) 11, 49, 105, 110, 120, 132
Plaza de Armas 48, 72, 74
political policy 36–37
pollution: air 50, 52, 57, 59; control 62, 67, 82, 131
population: growth 5, 20, 32, 36, 40, 48, 95, 105; reduction 4
poverty 5, 13, 26, 57, 92, 96, 98, 107
power: generation of 79, 82, 87; plant 55

PPI's (private participation in infrastructure) 37
productivity 13, 26, 37, 50, 68, 80, 104, 117, 123
public: health 6, 33, 43, 56, 66, 73, 102, 104–105; policy 118; space 11, 17, 21, 26, 41, 98, 117, 120, 124

quality of life: defined as 49; increased 3, 47, 58, 61, 68, 83, 103, 119, 125; opportunities 81
Quintero, Daniel 117, 124

Rayner, Geof 102
research and development (R&D) 124–125
research findings 21, 83–84, 118
residential: dwelling units 22, 77; energy consumption 73, 77, 80–81
resilient: city 3, 132; environment 3, 12, 80
resource: local 3; management 1, 34–35, 37, 61; natural 26, 50
respiratory disease 12, 49–50, 52, 57, 79
responsibility 2, 68, 97
Rimac River 47

safety issues 2, 6, 20–22, 27, 64, 107, 119
sanitation 48, 91, 131
Santiago: energy consumption and sustainability 72, 76, 79–80; energy sources **78**, *82, 85*; initiatives 81, 86; settlement development 74
Santiago Local Energetic Strategy 76
Santiago Transportation Master Plan 81
Santos, Juan Manuel 113, 117
school: abandonment (dropout) 19; public 2, 9, 109, 130
science, technology, and innovation (STI) 124–125
Secretary of Economic Development 124
Secretary of Energy 76, 78, 84
Secretary of Environment **51**, 62, 98
Secretary of Justice 76
Secretary of Mobility 24
Secretary of Social Development 91, 97
segregation 5, 10–11, 26, 75, 116
settlements 17, 26, 48–49, 92, 96, 107
sewage 8, 14, 18, 37, 40, 47–48, 74
slums 49, 95
social: behaviour 103; capital 11, 14, 22, 120; equity 2, 13, 27, 43, 68, 120, 125; frustrations 8; inequity 6, 49; justice 2, 80, 87, 98, 106, 114, 126, 130; transformation 7, 113–114
social mobility: built environment and 8, 11, 18; opportunity **19**; tools 12–13
socioeconomic: groups 13, 18–19, 76; ladder 6, 13, 19, 27; status 11, 21
solar: energy 79, 83–84; panels 42, 78, 84, 86
Spanish crown 1, 47–48, 74
streetcar/trolley 8
sulfur dioxide (SO2) 55–56, 58, 79
survey: results 6, 9, 13, 21, **23**; urban living questionnaire 21
Surveys on Social Mobility in Mexico 13
Sustainable Energy Agency 76

technology 40, 68, 98, 114
Territorial Organizational Plat (POT) 17, 26
trade 5, 95, 105, 107, 131
traffic: congestion 3, 52–53, 62, 64, 81; control 65–66; lights/signals 62, 64–65
tramway 48, 73
transformation 2, 4, 122, 126, 132; *see also* social transformation
transportation: car, dependency on 50, 64; public 9, 27, 42, 52, 60, 82, 119–120, 131; railway 36, 42, 64–65, 75, 95, 116; ride-share systems 64–65, 82; sector 49, 52, 55, 61, 77, 80–81, 84; underground 5, 95

Index 139

undernourishment 101, **102**; *see also* malnutrition
United Nations: Economic Commission for Latin America 4, 63; Sustainable Development Goals 98
United States 1, 4, 10, 19, 58, 72
urban: footprint 17, 41, 75, 105, 109–110; infrastructure 17, 20, 49, 62; laboratories 5; planning 22, 49, 81, 92, 110, 130–131; sprawl 8, 10, 14
urban agriculture: programs 91, 98, 100, 109; zoning and land use 105–106
Urban Development National Policy (PNDU) 75–76
Urban Growth and Access to Opportunities 22
urbanization 6, 48–49, 105
urbanized 4, 14, 17
utility pricing 18

Valdivia, Pedro de 74
value: adding/increased 4, 64, 84; home, real-estate 17–18, 37, 63
violence 8, 46
vision (future) 3–5, 27, 61, 81, 118, 123, 126

waste: disposal 47, 51–52; management 18, 49, 51, 66
water: consumption 38, 43; contamination 33, 40, 48; equal access **35**, 38, 40; infrastructure **35**, 37–38, 103; management 34, **35**, 40, 43, 51; potable 34, 39–42, 91; pricing 37; quality 34, 37, 39; scarcity 3, 6, 43, 79; storage/recycling 36, 40, 43; sustainability 37–38, 62; technology 40, 42–43; waste water treatment 62
water supply 6, 31, 36, 38, 131
wealth accumulation 11–12, 17, 22, 130
white flight 10
World Air Quality Index 52
World Bank 37, 87, 121
World Coal Association 79
World Cup 75
World Energy Council 81
World Health Organization (WHO) 31, 38, 49–50, 55–57, 62, 106
World War (I & II) 1, 95

zoning 2, 11–12, 20, 86, 92, 105, 110, 120

For Product Safety Concerns and Information please contact our EU
representative GPSR@taylorandfrancis.com
Taylor & Francis Verlag GmbH, Kaufingerstraße 24, 80331 München, Germany

www.ingramcontent.com/pod-product-compliance
Lightning Source LLC
Chambersburg PA
CBHW051750230426
43670CB00012B/2234